Faith of Our Fathers

Faith of Our Fathers

Why the Early Christians Still Matter and Always Will

---

by Mike Aquilina
with an introduction by David Mills

EMMAUS
ROAD
PUBLISHING

Steubenville, Ohio
A Division of Catholics United for the Faith
www.emmausroad.org

EMMAUS
ROAD
PUBLISHING

Emmaus Road Publishing
827 North Fourth Street
Steubenville, Ohio 43952

Library of Congress Control Number: 2012950283
ISBN: 978-1-937155-87-2

Cover design and layout by Julie Davis, General Glyphics, Inc., Dallas, Texas

Cover art: The Four Doctors of the Church with the Symbols of the Four Evangelists. 1516.
Sacchi, Pier Francesco (1485-1528). Photo Credit:© RMN-Grand Palais / Art Resource, NY.

DEDICATION

TO CARDINAL DONALD WUERL
in gratitude for all he's done for the Church
and for my loved ones

ACKNOWLEDGMENTS

MOST OF THESE PIECES GOT STARTED because some editor had a great idea. Almost all of them got done because some editor reminded me of a deadline. I'd like to thank those editors: Msgr. Owen Campion, Bill Cone, Bill Dodds, Joyce Duriga, Michael Hahn, Gerry Korson, Bob Lockwood, David Mills, Sarah Rozman, David Scott, Michael Steier, Mike Sullivan. God bless them all for their love of the Fathers—and for consistently making me look smarter than I am.

I acknowledge their estimable publications, too, for deigning to publish my work: *Catholic Heritage, Catholic New World, Lay Witness, Our Sunday Visitor, Pittsburgh Catholic, The Priest,* and *Touchstone.*

I am grateful especially to Mike Sullivan for bringing this book to press and to my beloved godson David Mills for contributing the introduction (which is my favorite part of the book).

Thanks be to my wife, who bought me the Catholic University of America edition of the Fathers, so many years ago, and got this whole thing started. Thanks be to God, from whom all blessings flow.

CONTENTS

INTRODUCTION

BY DAVID MILLS

ONE CHILD WHISPERS TO ANOTHER, the message going from Jenny to Bobby to John to Mungo and on to the bright and chipper little girl who always seems to be sitting in the last chair, till she tells everyone what she heard, which is not what the teacher had whispered to the first child. We've all played this game in grade school, with the same result. My sixth grade teacher, knowing sixth graders, had promised some fabulous prize to the class if we could get the message right, but we couldn't. We didn't come close. I still remember the collective groan and the look on the little girl's face when she realized she'd delivered bad news rather than good.

It's a useful lesson in what happens when people try to pass on a message. I think of it whenever someone says that we should submit ourselves to the Church fathers because they wrote just one hundred or two hundred or four hundred years after the Resurrection. They were so close to Jesus and the Apostles, they must have gotten it right. From them we'll get the real story, pure and undefiled. They were right there, or anyway, they were almost right there.

But they really weren't. They were sitting where John or Mungo were sitting. If kids trying their hardest to pass on the exact words can't manage to do it in five minutes, how can we expect dozens or hundreds of very different people over decades or centuries to do it?

Who knows how much the message had changed along the way? Who knows how much of the story had been changed and polished and refined till it sounded just right, the way urban legends develop as people revise the stories to make them say what they feel they should say. After a while, everyone who hears the stories thinks they must be true, because, you know, they just sound right. They sound right only because almost everyone who told it helped make it sound right.

This is the argument skeptical scholars have been making against the Fathers for two hundred years or so. They insist that no group of people could have kept the message straight over that much time, and that the early Christians would naturally have changed the story to make it sound better to them. What we think of as Christian teaching, they say, is really a kind of ancient urban legend.

Some of these scholars, for example, decided that as the early Christians passed on the original pure message of grace and freedom they added all the laws and structures we now think of as part of life in the Church, because they needed rules, and they needed rulers. They couldn't live without crutches, so they put them into the story. The modern scholars called this retreat from what Jesus wanted "early Catholicism." All that doctrine, all those bishops, all that morality, that wasn't what Jesus had taught, but what frightened or lazy Christians had inserted into the story as they passed it along.

This way of thinking about the Fathers became the academic standard, and remains so today. If you study the Fathers, you assume that they came to believe what they believed because they believed many of the same things as everyone else they knew and they revised the beliefs they'd received to make them more enjoyable. You don't read them as authorities but as people who helped create or refine an urban legend.

You also believe that their beliefs were only one alternative among the early Christians and not necessarily the obvious choice to survive. They won the arguments, sometimes by using the state to enforce their will, and so the average Christian today naively assumes that they were right. For these skeptics, all "orthodox Christianity" means is "the beliefs of the winners."

The modern scholarly skeptics are not the only ones who've downgraded the Fathers. Some aggressive Protestants have been making pretty much the same argument since the Reformation, but with a twist. They rejected the Fathers' teaching when it contradicted Protestant commitments, as when some of them wanted to reject the papacy and others wanted to reject bishops in general. In these cases, they argued that the Fathers had corrupted Scripture.

But they also accepted the Fathers, when they could push the teaching they liked back far enough to use the Fathers as if they were early Protestants. They often quoted Cyril of Jerusalem or Augustine on Scripture against what they insisted was the Church's corrupt elevation of Tradition over Scripture. They thought (and their descendents often think) that they were scoring points against the Catholic Church by taking away the Fathers that Catholics had used to defend and explain the teachings at stake in the Reformation.

The skeptics, it seems to me, have the better argument. The Protestants have a big problem trying to use Scripture against the Fathers, since the Fathers were the ones who preserved Scripture and decided which writings would become our Scriptures. You can't really argue that the Fathers knew what Scripture is yet didn't know how the Church should read it. They also have the problem that the very earliest Fathers said things they don't agree with, like Ignatius' teaching on the Eucharist, which is far more obviously Catholic than the average Protestant can tolerate. They can hardly justify claiming the authority of the second century Fathers against the Church without accepting it for themselves.

The skeptics, though, they have a good argument. We do know how beliefs change through history, the way a message changes as it's whispered from child to child to child. Anyone who's taken Sociology 101 knows that people's beliefs reflect their culture and society. Anyone who's paid attention to his friends and neighbors, or looked very carefully at his own life, knows that people often believe whatever they want, like the man who discovers that marriage is an oppressive institution the moment he falls in love with his secretary.

And even the greatest fan of the Church fathers has to admit that there were a lot of them and they didn't always agree, and some of them said some things the Church condemned. It's not always so easy to settle a question by declaring "The Fathers say," because someone else might point out that some of the ancients said this or that, while others said the opposite. Arius thought Jesus was God's first creation, and appealed to Scripture to support his view,

Athanasius insisted that Jesus was the eternally begotten Son of God, and both were priests in good standing at the time. Tertullian was wrong about Mary's perpetual virginity, and Jerome was right. Origen was wrong about the pre-existence of the soul and other matters as well.

So why read the Fathers? More to the point, why follow the men and women we call *the* Fathers? Why not read everyone from the early centuries and use the writers and the ideas we think the best ones? Why prefer Irenaeus to the Gnostics? Why choose Athanasius over Arius? Why listen to Augustine rather than Pelagius? Why not at least accept them all as different witnesses to the great mystery of God, some of whom will appeal to one person and others to another person. The rationalist may prefer Irenaeus, the new ager the Gnostics, and to each his own. Why be so dogmatically and tyrannically insistent on the authority of the official Church fathers?

That is the question Mike Aquilina answers in this book (parts of which, I am proud to say, I first published). Of course the Church has discerned within the Fathers' writing and passed on to us the Catholic faith, and strained out the errors, mistakes, and half-truths. But that might be just an argument for just sticking with the *Catechism of the Catholic Church* and reading the modern popes and leaving the Fathers for the scholars and the kind of dweebs—like Mike—who like that sort of thing.

What Mike shows in these essays is that the Fathers not only passed on to us the deep and life-changing truths of the Catholic faith that we now find articulated in more modern ways in the *Catechism*. They taught it with extraordinary wisdom and insight, and often with very illuminating examples and analogies, and with a superb sense of how the truths they were teaching worked in real life. Particularly, I want to say, how these truths can change your life in this world.

The other early Christian writers, the ones the scholars and the television networks love, simply don't do this. You will not find in the *Gospel of Thomas* or (the latest sensation) the *Gospel of Judas*, anything of comparable depth and insight. For the most part, you get some obscure stories with a lot of sayings of the sort you'd hear from a new age stoner.

For example, from the Gnostic tract *Thunder, Perfect Mind*: "For I am the first and the last I am the honored one and the scorned one. I am the whore and the holy one. I am the wife and the virgin. . . .I am the silence that is incomprehensible and the idea whose remembrance is frequent." This isn't really very helpful as a religious statement, at least one that will help the average person, who doesn't sit around in a circle thinking deep thoughts and occasionally smacking his forehead and saying "Wow!"

Compare this with the opening of the second chapter of Athanasius's *On the Incarnation*. Athanasius begins with the fact that man is dying. Man, he writes, "created in God's image and in his possession of reason reflected the very Word Himself, was disappearing, and the work of God was being undone." This is a problem for us, obviously, but it's also a problem for God, if I may put it that way, because God is good and just.

> *It would, of course, have been unthinkable that God should go back upon His word and that man, having transgressed, should not die; but it was equally monstrous that beings which once had shared the nature of the Word should perish and turn back again into non-existence through corruption. It was unworthy of the goodness of God that creatures made by Him should be brought to nothing through the deceit wrought upon man by the devil; and it was supremely unfitting that the work of God in mankind should disappear, either through their own negligence or through the deceit of evil spirits. As, then, the creatures whom He had created reasonable, like the Word, were in fact perishing, and such noble works were on the road to ruin, what then was God, being Good, to do?*

This may seem like a question for theologians, but it is an intensely practical question for all of us, who are in fact dying, physically and spiritually. In the rest of his short book, Athanasius answers the question in a way that illuminates the Incarnation, giving us some idea of why God became man and what it means for us.

On the Incarnation thus extends the Gospel, the good news. It doesn't change it. It's not one stage in the creation of an urban legend. It draws out for us in ways we can understand what Jesus said and did and what the Scriptures mean. That is one way to define the work of the Fathers: They took the Gospel and ran with it, and brought it to us with its meaning laid out more clearly and its truth made even more compelling and powerful.

In this book, Mike Aquilina shows us in detail how the Fathers ran with the Gospel, to our eternal benefit. Learning what the Fathers have to teach us is the best answer to the question, Why follow the Fathers? The proof is in the pudding.

David Mills is executive editor of First Things magazine and author of *Discovering Mary: Answers to Questions About the Mother of God*, *The Saints' Guide to Knowing the Real Jesus*, and *The Pilgrim's Guide: C. S. Lewis and the Art of Witness*.

THE FATHERS AS TEACHERS

(AND TEACHERS OF TEACHERS)

THERE IS TODAY A GREAT DEAL OF CURIOSITY about the earliest years of Christianity. We see it whenever a bestselling novel proposes an alternative story line (or bloodline) for the Church's origins. We see it whenever an archeologist turns up a previously unknown apocryphal gospel—and the news media say that it calls everything into question. We see it in the cottage industries that have grown up around the study of the Dead Sea Scrolls and the Gnostic gospels, not to mention the works of the early Church fathers. There are now about half a dozen multi-volume series, in print, of the works of the Fathers.

Why should this concern us as we approach the work of catechesis? Well, for many reasons.

First, it should concern us because it's of interest to a large and growing segment of the people we're called to serve—the people we want to reach. Somebody's buying those books and magazines. Somebody's tuning into those documentaries on The History Channel. All those somebodies are people hungry for catechesis, even if they don't know it. Even if they think they're just curious about history.

Second, the Fathers should concern us because they managed to pull off an amazing achievement. They converted the pagan world in a mere two and a half centuries. They did it without any resources, without any social or political power. They did it with the most primitive communications media. Yet their Church sustained a steady growth rate of forty percent per decade over the course of those centuries. Maybe there's something we can learn from them.

Finally, the Fathers answer to a deep human need—a need for roots. The fascination with early Christianity is a lot like the widespread, more general interest in genealogy. The early Christians are our ancestors. In fact, the Greek and Latin word for "Fathers" means ancestors, too. Those folks with the uncommon names—Perpetua, Polycarp, Aphrahat—are details of our common genealogy. They're family to us, in the communion of saints. We have a common mother in the Church; and they do share our bloodline, since they and we have shared holy communion in the blood of Jesus Christ.

Getting to know the Fathers means getting to know our own roots. It means knowing more deeply who we are as we learn more and more about who they are.

When we see them in icons, the early Christians may seem exotic, remote, and essentially different from you and me. But as we allow ourselves to enter their world, by way of study and by way of our imagination, we learn that they're not so different. We share a common humanity, of course. But, more than that, we share a common Christianity—a Catholic faith that is recognizable across the millennia.

So we see men and women who love the Mass. Who make the Sign of the Cross. Who go to Confession. Who use holy water. Who ask the intercession of the saints, and who offer Mass for the dead. We see a familiar hierarchy of pope, bishop, priest, and deacon. We find devout souls who love to call their Church "catholic."

So let's take our first steps into that world—our first steps on a tour where our guides are the Fathers (and Mothers, too) of the Church.

THE FATHERS AS TEACHERS

LET'S BEGIN BY ASKING: Who are the Fathers?

They're a select group of teachers from the early Church. Right away, we should be interested, because they're teachers like us. We share with them the mission of catechesis.

What's more, they're the cream of the crop.

When we speak of "the Fathers," we're talking not about everyone who held a teaching office in the Church, or everyone whose writings have survived. Nor are we talking about the smartest theologians, or the nicest or most well-behaved people.

We're talking about an elite, an exclusive group of around a hundred authors whom Catholic tradition has held up for veneration as somehow "Fatherly" to all Christians of all ages.

That's quite an elite—just a hundred teachers from a span of seven hundred years. When we read the Fathers, we're reading the best of the best.

Consider what it took for their teaching to survive even the course of their own lifetime. There were no printing presses and no electronic media. So their books and sermons and letters had to be duplicated in longhand. Copying a long book might be a month's work for a scribe—and the work of a scribe was very expensive.

The books were copied onto papyrus or parchment—not the most durable media. There was no such thing as acid-free paper. So the materials tended to rot away quickly.

And then the books had to survive not only the elements and the ravages of time—but also the laws of imperial persecutors. It was, at various times, a serious crime to own Christian books. What the authorities found, they destroyed. Sometimes, too, Christians destroyed the evidence or buried it in order to reduce exposure to danger.

So the Fathers are those teachers whose works—whose teaching—has survived a millennium and more, and against all odds. Remember the old hymn: The "faith of our fathers," even in its written form, is "living still in spite of dungeon, fire, and sword."

That tells us something about the value of the Fathers' works. People were willing to spend a great deal of money—and risk their lives—to copy them out laboriously and preserve them. And this had to happen not just in one generation, but several times per generation, and then several times in every succeeding generation afterward, for hundreds of years. Time functioned as a great sieve, allowing only the finest material to survive.

THE TEACHING OF THE FATHERS, then, has proven over time to be well worth learning.

Yet, as I said earlier, not every early Christian author is considered a Church father. What sets the elite group apart from a pack that includes many other intelligent, gifted, and able authors?

Four things set these men apart from those who would seem to be their peers in many respects:

1. Holiness of life
2. Soundness of doctrine
3. Church approval
4. Antiquity

Those are the four qualities the Church looks for in designating an author to be a "Father."

1. HOLINESS OF LIFE. In Latin, the word is Sanctitas, which we translate as "sanctity" or even "sainthood." Thus, most of the Fathers are canonized saints whose memorials you'll find on the Church's calendar—the folks whose names begin with "St."
2. SOUNDNESS OF DOCTRINE. In the ancient languages, they spoke of orthodoxia, orthodoxy. In English, this has an intellectual ring to it. We tend to think of doctrine in terms of propositions. But at root "orthodoxy" means more than sound thinking. It means "right praise." It meant you could worship with the Church because you believed with the Church.
3. CHURCH APPROVAL. There is no canonization process for Church-Fatherhood. So how does this approval take place? Well, the Fathers are those who have been quoted authoritatively, down the years, by the councils and revered teachers. If you were cited as an ancient authority by the Council of Ephesus in AD 431, or the Council of Chalcedon in 451, or the Second Vatican Council in 1965, then you have Church approval.

4. ANTIQUITY. Today, when we speak of "antiquity," we mean a specific period that we call the Age of the Fathers, or the Patristic Era. It stretches from the first century through the eighth century. For the Fathers themselves, though, antiquity was a relative term. For St. Irenaeus, writing in the late 100s, antiquity encompassed the lifetime of the man who had baptized him—St. Polycarp, who was a disciple of St. John the Apostle. Antiquity means these men have stood the test of time. There's no chance whatsoever that they represent a passing theological or devotional fad. They belong to the ages.

THE STUDY OF THE CHURCH FATHERS actually began in the era of the Church fathers. The Fathers themselves were intensely interested in their forebears in the Faith. In the second century, St. Irenaeus set down his recollections of St. Polycarp. As the third century drew to a close, Eusebius traveled from city to city to scour the churches' archives for their most ancient sources. He quoted these extensively in his massive Ecclesiastical History. In the mid-fourth century, St. Jerome composed a great encyclopedia of Illustrious Men from apostolic times to his own day.

Around the same time, St. Helena, the mother of the Emperor Constantine, and St. Ambrose, the bishop of Milan, made the first ventures in Christian archeology, excavating sites related to the life of Christ and the deaths of the martyrs. On that holy ground they built basilicas that provided a catechesis of sorts, teaching pilgrims through the media of stone and bone, mosaic and fresco.

St. Augustine delighted in preaching on the feasts of his ancestors in the Faith. He learned from their words and their lives, and he desired nothing more for himself and his flock than fidelity to the ancient models. In AD 421 he said of those who had gone before him in faith: "They held to what they found in the Church. They taught what they had learned. What they had received from the Fathers, they passed on to the children."[1]

That essential task of preservation was carried out in the councils as well, where the bishops usually appended a catena—or chain—of quotations from the Fathers as evidence of the antiquity of the councils' dogmatic conclusions.

---

1 St. Augustine, *Contra Julianum* 2.9.

In the fifth century—still in the era of the Fathers—we find some first attempts to approach the ancients in a systematic way. There is a list of approved authors and works usually attributed to Pope Gelasius I. The great authority on the study of Christian antiquity, however, is St. Vincent of Lerins, a monk of fifth-century Gaul, the land now known as France. Vincent set down rules for the study of the Fathers: "Now in the Catholic Church, we take the greatest care to hold what has been believed everywhere, always and by all ... the bishops and teachers of antiquity."[2]

Yet, as we know, antiquity alone does not bestow authority. Remember, there are those four marks of a Father, and antiquity is only one of them. Indeed, it is from Vincent that the theologians of the Church have drawn those four marks. For Vincent wrote that "the opinions of those Fathers only are to be used for comparison, who lived and taught in a way that was holy, wise, and constantly in communion, and were counted worthy either to die in the faith of Christ, or to suffer death happily for Christ."[3]

So it is from the early Christians that we learned to place a premium on history, tradition, and fidelity to what has been handed down to us. It is a trait the Christian Fathers share with the rabbis of early rabbinic Judaism. History matters much to people whose faith rests on historical covenants, historical events.

Those early efforts of Eusebius, Jerome, and Vincent have borne great fruit through the ages, and have developed into many specialized sub-disciplines within the field of theology.

Patristics is what we call the study of the theological doctrine of the Fathers.

Patrology is the study of the life and writings of the Fathers.

Today, many people use these two terms interchangeably. The root of both is pater, a word that means "father" or "ancestor" in both the Greek and Latin languages.

The terms have become interchangeable because the lives of the Fathers are inseparable from the development of their doctrine, and their lives are illustrative of their doctrine.

---

2   St. Vincent of Lerins, *Commonitory* 2.6.

3   *Ibid.*, 28.72.

IN THEOLOGY AND IN THE LIFE OF THE CHURCH, the Fathers have always stood as authorities. In recent centuries—especially since the Protestant Reformation—there have been many attempts to define more precisely what is the authority of the Fathers.

The Fathers, after all, are not divinely inspired like the Scriptures.

They do not enjoy the charism of infallibility as the popes do.

In fact, the Fathers sometimes disagree with one another.

On occasion ... they even bickered with one another.

- ▷ St. Cyril of Alexandria belonged to the party that deposed and exiled St. John Chrysostom from the see of Constantinople.
- ▷ St. Jerome thought St. Augustine was conniving and proud.
- ▷ St. Jerome accused St. Ambrose of plagiarism.
- ▷ St. Jerome thought St. John Chrysostom was overrated.

St. Jerome, as we can see, had some issues.

Yet he also has authority, as a Church father; and so do the saints who irritated him, the saints he sometimes opposed.

What exactly is that authority?

At the Council of Trent, the Church declared that any time we find a consensus of the Fathers on any point of doctrine or interpretation of Scripture, that point may not be opposed. This notion of the "consensus of the Fathers" was confirmed and expanded by the First Vatican Council.[4]

One of the men who took part in the Vatican Council, Blessed John Henry Newman, was a great scholar of the Fathers. And he held that the Fathers possess the authority not of judges, but of witnesses. He wrote: "We take them as honest informants, but not as sufficient authority in themselves, though they are an authority, too."[5]

The Fathers witness to something greater than themselves. They witness to the authority of the Church to which they submitted themselves in life.

In the twentieth century, a German theologian named Joseph Ratzinger took up again the question of the Fathers' authority. In his book Principles of Catholic Theology, he says that the Fathers have a constitutive role in Catholic

---

4   See Council of Trent, Session 4; Vatican I, *Dei Filius*.

5   Blessed John Henry Newman, "The Patristical Idea of Antichrist," Lecture II, in *Discussions and Arguments* (London: Longmans, Green, 1907), 45.

teaching.[6] They're part of our constitution. He goes on to explore what that role might be, and he concludes that it is an essential part of divine revelation.

For revelation, he explains, is communication, and communication is a two-way process. It requires a speaker and a listener . . . a call and a response. God's revelation was perfect and complete in His Word, Jesus Christ our Lord. Nevertheless, His Word awaited a reception—an acceptance—an Amen on the part of the Church.

The era of the Fathers—and the lives and works and deaths of those Fathers—represented the Church's constitutional Amen to God's definitive revelation.

How did the Fathers express it?

They did it in many ways:

▷ by setting a stable canon of Scripture
▷ by setting down the classic creeds
▷ by establishing the ritual and sacramental life of the Church . . . founding the great liturgical families . . . by baptizing, absolving, anointing, and offering the Eucharist everywhere on earth.
▷ by modeling the discipline, order, and morals that were proper to God's New Covenant people
▷ by preserving the proper hierarchical roles of all members of the Church, those in orders, those in consecrated life, and those in the laity
▷ and by living the Gospel in a way that established a model for all ages

Thus we look to them as witnesses even today, and so they are invoked in the Catechism of the Catholic Church.

The Catechism lists the Fathers second among its principal sources, right after Scripture and right before the liturgy (n. 11).

The Catechism tells us that the Fathers are "always timely witnesses" to the Church's tradition (n. 688).

To those who hold some teaching office, the Catechism holds the Fathers up as models, master teachers. "Periods of renewal in the Church are also intense moments of catechesis. In the great era of the Fathers of the Church, saintly bishops devoted an important part of their ministry to catechesis. St. Cyril of Jerusalem and St. John Chrysostom, St. Ambrose and St. Augustine,

---

6   Joseph Ratzinger, *Principles of Catholic Theology: Building Stones for a Fundamental Theology* (San Francisco: Ignatius, 1987), 151-152. See also the discussion of Ratzinger's treatment of the Fathers in Aidan Nichols, O.P., *The Shape of Catholic Theology* (Collegeville, MN: Liturgical Press, 1991), 205-206.

and many other Fathers wrote catechetical works that remain models for us" (n. 8).

THE FATHERS "REMAIN MODELS FOR US." And they provide many different sorts of models. There should be no one who says that the Fathers as a whole are just "not my style." For the Fathers modeled many different styles and methods of teaching.

When we speak of the Fathers, we're talking about a very diverse group, spread over many cultures and using many languages, in a variety of secular circumstances.

Sometimes categorizing the Fathers helps us to home in on the ancient authors who will be most useful to us, and most congenial to our own reading habits and interests. Sometimes dividing them helps us to search out the authors who performed best at the task we struggle with today—whether it's explaining the Trinity, or defending the mission of the Church, or understanding human nature.

Since the Church faced different sets of concerns in different periods, sometimes it's helpful to divide the Fathers by time period.

The earliest group is the Apostolic Fathers. These men lived in the first century and early second century, and their lives overlapped with the lives of the Apostles. Some were probably disciples of the Apostles. The title of "Apostolic Father" is usually given to Pope St. Clement I, whose Letter to the Corinthians survives; St. Ignatius of Antioch, a bishop and martyr, whose seven letters survive; and St. Polycarp of Smyrna, another bishop and martyr, whom we know from one brief letter and a biography composed by his secretary. The Apostolic Fathers are primarily concerned about issues of order and discipline within the Church and the morals of the Church's members.

The next group is called the Ante-Nicene (or Pre-Nicene) Fathers. They take us through the remainder of the second century and all of third century, up to the time Christianity was legalized in AD 313. They are a sizeable group, whose stellar names include Justin Martyr, Melito of Sardis, Irenaeus of Lyons, Tertullian of Carthage, Hippolytus of Rome, Clement of Alexandria, Origen of Alexandria, Cyprian of Carthage, and many others. This period also introduces the earliest known Christian woman writer, Perpetua of

Carthage, who left us her prison journal. The Ante-Nicene Fathers address a wider range of concerns, including the proliferation of heresies within and at the edges of Christianity; the intensification of the imperial persecution of the Church; and the attacks upon Christian doctrine by pagan philosophers and statesmen.

The third age of the Fathers we call the Nicene and Post-Nicene Age. The Fathers of this period were defined by their participation in the first ecumenical council, the Council of Nicaea, or in the gradual working-out of Nicaea's doctrine. These labors lasted for centuries and required clarification at subsequent ecumenical councils—at Constantinople in 381, Ephesus in 431, Chalcedon in 451, and in three other councils before the end of the Patristic era. The councils settled important questions regarding the natures and person of Jesus Christ and the dogma of the Trinity. The leading lights of this period were Athanasius, Basil the Great, Ephrem of Syria, Gregory of Nazianzus, Gregory of Nyssa, Hilary of Poitiers, Ambrose of Milan, Augustine of Hippo, Leo the Great, Gregory the Great, Maximus Confessor, John of Damascus, and many, many others.

In this period, the Church moved from persecution to imperial favor—and then imperial monopoly. This raised new questions about the relationship between Church and state, and the Fathers engaged those questions in a variety of ways. As this period drew to a close, lands that had been officially Christian began falling to Islam in the Arab invasions.

The Fathers can also be divided by cultural or language groups.

▷ Most of the early Fathers wrote in Greek, even those who labored in Rome, like Clement and Hippolytus.

▷ The Latin Fathers include the later writers of North Africa, Italy, Spain, and Gaul.

▷ The Syriac Fathers wrote in a language (and culture) that had many similarities to Jesus' own. They include such great teachers as Aphrahat the Sage and Ephrem the Deacon.

▷ The Coptic Fathers include the famous "athletes of prayer" from the Egyptian wilderness, the Desert Fathers.

▷ There are also Armenian Fathers, Georgian Fathers, and Ethiopic Fathers who wrote in Amharic.

We may categorize the Fathers according to their literary genres. There are . . .

▷ Apologists—who explained and defended the Faith.

▷ Exegetes—who interpreted the Scriptures.

▷ Historians—who preserved archival material and left written accounts of important events.

▷ Preachers—who composed and delivered memorable homilies and meditations.

▷ Hymnographers—who enriched worship with their liturgical music and verses.

▷ Catechists—who gave instruction in basic doctrine as well as the deepest mysteries.

▷ And spiritual writers—who gave counsel on Christian prayer, charity, and morals.

Of course, some of the Fathers were very prolific, and one genre cannot adequately contain their works. A polymath like Origen could produce seminal works on apologetics, prayer, and biblical interpretation. In the case of Augustine, it's hard to think of a genre he didn't master. He might even have invented a few!

WHEN WE THINK OF "TEACHERS" TODAY, we imagine people working in brick-and-mortar schools—with classrooms, mass-produced books, and very young students segregated by age. But there is little evidence that any such institutions existed in the age of the early Fathers. In those early centuries, persecution would have made such gatherings difficult or impossible.

What's more, there were no printing presses, so there were no textbooks, no catechisms, no worksheets. Remember, literacy was rare. Classroom schooling was for the privileged few. Yet Christianity was then, as it was in the time of James Joyce, and as it continues to be today: "Here Comes Everybody."

So we should not think of the Fathers as academics—pondering obscure points of angelology among their fellow scholars. They were primarily pastors, and most of their works represent the Church's pastoral response to urgent local circumstance.

With no printing presses and no schools, the Church's ordinary medium was the liturgical assembly. The Fathers did much of their teaching when their people came to Mass.

They aimed their teaching at adults, assuming that parents would pass the Catholic faith on to their children. And they tried to convey the important details in memorable ways—through hymns, for example, or prayers, or poems, or brief slogans.

In the early years, a parish "church" was rarely a dedicated building. The church met for Mass in the homes of believers. Sometimes these homes were decorated with artwork that depicted biblical scenes or images of the martyrs. These images, too, served a catechetical purpose, cultivating a Christian imagination in congregations that could not afford the luxury of literacy.

The heart of the early Fathers' teaching was the so-called "rule of faith," a brief, creed-like summary of doctrine. Though the wording varied from place to place, the formulas were remarkably consistent in content. They proclaimed that God became man in Jesus Christ, whose life had been foretold by the prophets; and that Christ died, rose from the dead, and is now glorified. Eventually, these formulas developed into the uniform baptismal creeds that we recite even today.

Baptisms took place at Easter, and the run-up to Holy Week was a time of intensive teaching addressed especially to newcomers to the practice of the Faith. The Fathers used the most basic touchstones as their course outlines. They would walk petition by petition through the Our Father, article by article through the Creed, commandment by commandment through the Decalogue. Remarkably, they conveyed a constant sense of the divine origin of the doctrine, even as they spoke frankly of its practical consequences for everyday living.

At the same time, most of the Fathers observed a scrupulous silence regarding sacramental doctrine. Today we call this practice the "discipline of the secret." Those who were not yet baptized were not allowed to attend the sacramental rites. To go to Mass was to enter the holy of holies—the place of God's presence—and this was reserved for Jesus Christ, the Son of God, and all those who had come to share His life through baptism.

Catechesis of new Christians after baptism focused on the sacramental rites, walking through them step by step and explaining the meaning of the symbols, the words, the postures and gestures. This sort of teaching is known as mystagogy, or guidance in the mysteries, pedagogy for the hidden things.

Mystagogy was perhaps the most crucial phase of catechesis for the Fathers. Sacramental communion was the goal—the earthly foretaste of heavenly glory that made sense of the Church's moral teaching. Though moral teaching often preceded mystagogy, the sacramental teaching brought it to a certain completion. The last material in completion was the first in intention. For the Fathers, the moral law was ordered to the liturgy. The Fathers taught their people to live their lives in a way that disposed each of them to the fullness of divine love.

The Church's magisterium has recently urged us all to take up this task once again, and learn from the Fathers, and revive the practice of mystagogy in the Church—not just for new Christians, but for all. This call is stated most urgently in Pope Benedict XVI's Sacramentum Caritatis and in the Catechism of the Catholic Church.

The Fathers are thus, once again, excellent models and timely witnesses for us. The fourth-century pilgrim Egeria tells us that when St. Cyril of Jerusalem delivered his mystagogical sermons, his listeners regularly interrupted him with thunderous applause. Surely the same was true in the churches of the other great mystagogues whose sermons have come down to us: Ambrose, Chrysostom, Augustine, and Theodore of Mopsusestia. If we read them today, we can understand why.

WE SHOULD NOTE, BY WAY OF EXCEPTION, that there were some institutional schools in the ancient Church. They were largely for adults, though occasionally attended by adolescent prodigies. And they were primarily for the training of Church leaders and highly motivated believers. Thus they were closer, in mission, to our modern seminaries or religious houses of formation. (Again, it was assumed that religious education of children would take place in the context of the liturgy and in the home.)

In the mid-second century, St. Justin Martyr traveled from his native Palestine to Rome, so that he could establish a school there. He taught a winsome Christian philosophy, informed by the classics he knew from his early training, and he succeeded in attracting many pupils. His success aroused the envy of pagan competitors, who denounced him as a Christian. He died willingly as a martyr, along with some of his pupils.

Just a few years later in Egypt arose the famous "Catechetical School" of Alexandria. St. Pantaenus is the first known rector. None of his works have survived, but we have much from two of his successors, St. Clement of Alexandria and Origen.

Clement's surviving works seem to be his lecture notes—or perhaps transcripts of his lectures—and he is clearly addressing a gathering of adults. He alludes often to the great works of pagan literature, the epic poems, the histories, and recent trends in philosophy. His audience is obviously deeply cultured and probably wealthy. Alexandria was the world's great center of research and trade at the end of the second century. Its intellectuals played among a multicultural and religious hash of ideas from Greece and India and Israel, not to mention the Pharaohs. Clement could engage the ideas in an intelligent way and give an intelligent Christian response. He was likely appealing to what we would today call religious "seekers" among the city's elites.

Among the institutional "schools" we should perhaps mention the circle of Roman noblewomen who were disciples of St. Jerome. They mastered the biblical languages under his tutelage—and some of them surpassed their teacher. He envied their ability to speak Hebrew without an accent. Some of them moved to the holy land, all for the sake of their biblical studies.

In the fourth century, we encounter many groups gathered for the sake of study conducted in a setting of common prayer. Chrysostom belonged to such a household of friends in Antioch. Aphrahat did, too, in the land now known as Iraq; as did Augustine in northern Italy.

Once ordained, Chrysostom placed a premium on adult education. In addition to his usual liturgical homilies, he also delivered series of sermons. Sometimes he offered a spiritual perspective on current events and crises. Other times he just walked through the books of the Bible, line by line, explaining and commenting as he went along. He was a trained speaker, and he always prepared very well. To the people of Antioch, and later Constantinople, his preaching was the best entertainment in town—serious competition for the Sunday sporting events. He even complained about people who came to his liturgy but left in droves after the homily, to go out to the games.

THOSE EXCELLENT SCHOOLS WERE, nevertheless, exceptional. For the most part, the Fathers carried out their educational program by creating a liturgical culture—a ritual culture that enabled people to steep in the Faith, soak in it, absorb it.

The calendar was crucial. There were the biblical feasts that told the story of salvation history again and again. There were the memorials of the apostles and martyrs, which preserved the Church's history and held up examples for imitation. There was the lectionary, which presented the Scriptures every Sunday to great crowds of people who, over the course of a lifetime, would never be able to own or read a single book.

There were the sacramental milestones: like initiation at Easter, which was an annual, exhilarating experience of renewal and growth, not only for the newcomers, but for the whole community that stood and watched.

There were processions and vigils and pilgrimages. These were solemn, but they were festive, too. They were memorable in a sensory way. They made it a pleasure for people to remember the small details of their salvation.

There was holy water at the entrance to the church, and it was blessed by the priests to remind people of their baptism. This is attested by Eusebius of Caesarea in Palestine and Serapion of Egypt.

There was biblical and sacramental art on the walls and at the tombs.

There were the homilies, of course, but there were also the hymns that stayed in your head and on your lips long after the sermon was forgotten. The hymns and songs of Clement, Hilary, Ambrose, Ephrem, Prudentius—these were profoundly biblical. They taught clear doctrine. They read well as poetry, in the original or in translation. They resound even today, in modern settings. We Catholics should be ashamed to discover that the Fathers' lyrics appear more often in the hymnals of the Lutheran and Anglican churches than in our own.

Through these means and many others, the Fathers catechized. They had to accommodate a congregation of non-readers. They had to do it without books. So they used the media they had at hand and they exploited it to the full.

And they succeeded in raising up congregations—churches—that were seriously engaged in the Faith.

Try to imagine this: In the late fourth century, St. Gregory of Nyssa complained that ordinary people were spending too much time talking about theology. He said: "Mere youths and tradesmen, off-hand dogmatists in theology, servants too, and slaves that have been flogged ... are solemn with us and philosophical about things incomprehensible ... If you ask for change someone philosophizes to you on the begotten and the unbegotten."[7] And the problem followed poor Gregory wherever he went in the marketplace. If he asked the baker the price of his bread, he got Trinitarian doctrine instead. If he asked whether the bath was ready, he got still more.

Poor Gregory! ... No, poor us! Reading his lines today is like listening to someone complain about having too much money or a spouse who cooks too well.

We should hope to be half as successful as the Fathers in the way we teach our children (and our grownups).

WE SHOULD LEARN FROM THE FATHERS. We should at least adopt their attitude—a disposition of trust in God, a certain knowledge that heaven has a plan, and we're part of it—that Christ loves everyone in our diocese and longs for a holy communion with all of them—that we ourselves can do all things in Christ who strengthens us for the work of catechesis.

It was a paternal attitude. They were Fathers because God is a Father—and they had become partakers of his divine nature (2 Peter 1:4). They were Fathers because they, like St. Paul the Apostle, had been called to serve the family in a fatherly way.

St. Basil the Great referred to his bishop-predecessors as "the Fathers." And when he took office he said, "I myself have been appointed to the position of a father by reason of the station to which the Lord has appointed me."[8]

For a layman like Tertullian, the paternal sense came not when he received orders or an office, but it was there nonetheless. Nowhere is the "fatherhood" of the Fathers expressed more vividly than when that cantankerous man vigorously confronted heretics as poachers on his family's estate, trespassers who threatened his patrimony: "Who are you . . . Marcion, by what right do

7   St. Gregory of Nyssa, *On the Deity of the Son.*
8   St. Basil the Great, Letter 37.

you chop my wood? By whose permission, Valentinus, are you diverting my streams? By what power, Apelles, are you removing my boundary markers? This is my property . . . I hold sure title-deeds from the original owners themselves, to whom the estate belonged. I am the heir of the Apostles."[9]

Quite simply, their teaching shows a real parental care for the Church. In English we use the word "Fathers" to describe them; and in the ancient world they were mostly men. After all, women had limited educational opportunities available to them.

But we should not, for this reason, neglect the Church's ancient mothers.

Consider the case of the great Cappadocians. It is most often the men who get our attention: Basil the Great and Gregory of Nyssa. They were exemplary teachers, and they were teachers of teachers. In fact, Gregory of Nyssa wrote history's first comprehensive manual for catechists, his Great Catechism, anticipating Augustine's manuals by a generation.

Basil wrote rules of life and directed the studies of ascetical communities—and then adapted those principles to "monasticize" his city, to a limited extent.

These men had traveled abroad for their education, studying in Athens and at the capital. They had sat in the classrooms of the greatest orators of their day. They were Ivy League.

Yet they counted all that academic experience as nothing compared to what they had learned at home from their sister Macrina. Tradition calls her "Mother," and so she remains a "Mother of the Church" even today, and she cares for us as she cared for her siblings. But Gregory called her something else. He called her "The Teacher," employing the title employed by the New Testament and the Fathers to refer to Jesus Christ.

St. Macrina the Younger—mother and teacher in the Church—represents something radical and revolutionary in history. She was a woman in the ancient world. Yet, unlike other women, her identity depended not at all upon any mere man—not her father, not a husband, and not her sons, for she never married. She was a consecrated virgin, like tens of thousands of her contemporaries. She occupied an office unthinkable for a woman apart from Christianity.

She lived for Christ. And she attracted a community about her in Pontus, in Asia Minor. Her brothers in the priesthood, Basil and Gregory, served her sacramental needs. Yet she served them as spiritual Mother and Teacher.

---

9   Tertullian, *The Prescription Against Heretics* 37.

Gregory is renowned as a brilliant theologian. But he portrayed himself as her simple student, even at the end of her days, when she consoled him with a lesson on the doctrine of purgatory.

Such lessons are no less consoling today. This is the witness of the Fathers we can bring to our tasks right now. To the people we catechize, the antiquity of the Fathers is reassuring. It is solid. When we propose the seemingly incredible promises of Christianity, the Fathers show irrefutably that we're "not making this up." This isn't something we've invented. Brilliant people and good people have believed it all for centuries, from the time of the Apostles to this very morning.

In a world where everything's made to crumble, the Catholic faith is the only thing that lasts. The Seven Wonders of the Ancient World are ruins now, or they've vanished entirely, without a trace. Yet the Catholic faith prevails intact and with all the vigor of its youth. Nothing essential has been added. Nothing essential has been lost. And it's the only thing from the Roman Era that has survived.

There has been development, assuredly. In the fourth century, St. Basil showed that development is perfectly compatible with an unchanging faith. He said: "what now is mine has not taken the place of what existed in the beginning . . . Through progress we observe a certain amplification of what we say, which is not a change from worse to better, but is a completing of that which was lacking, according to the increment of our knowledge."[10]

The Fathers teach us humility before the Apostolic Tradition we have received. Their humility inspires us to want to learn more—and to share all that grace has given us to learn.

SO. VERY PRACTICALLY: What can we do differently or better now that we know the Fathers? What can we learn from them?

Here are a few things that I've learned and that I try to keep in mind in my own work and witness, with my family, in the neighborhood, and in the Church.

1. LOVE WHAT'S GOOD IN THE CULTURE. St. Justin Martyr looked for "seeds of the Word" everywhere in the world—in culture

10 St. Basil the Great, Letter 223.

and in current thought. We too should look for the places where we can meet people, affirm the good they do, and draw them closer to Christ. St. Justin also said that everything good is already ours. It already belongs to the one God, who is the Lord of all creation.

2. ISSUE A MORAL CHALLENGE. It's not enough for us to accentuate the positive. We must also reject the things that are sinful. The Fathers did not convert the Roman Empire by compromising with pagan morals. They spoke out against abortion, contraception, divorce, and the unjust use of military force. They brought an end to the culture of death by enabling the culture to become something better. With God's grace, we can do the same today.

3. USE THE MEDIA YOU HAVE. The Fathers didn't have much in the way of technology, but they used whatever they had. They wrote letters and poems. They wrote songs that taught doctrine and told Bible stories. They commissioned great artworks. But they also inscribed symbols of the Faith—a fish, a boat, an anchor—on common household items. They traveled. They preached. Today we have electronic media, not to mention good, old-fashioned books. Be creative.

4. BRING THE FATHERS INTO YOUR PRAYER AND STUDY. Read them. Read about them. If life allows you the privilege, make pilgrimage to the places where they walked. We live in a time when so much is available to us. St. Thomas Aquinas said he would trade all of Paris for a single volume of Chrysostom. We have hundreds of works by Chrysostom for free online—plus all the other ancient writers— and there are many accessible, popular books to help us learn from and pray with the Church's Fathers and Mothers.

5. BRING THE FATHERS INTO YOUR TEACHING. Share the things that excite you. Your excitement will be communicable. Show the icons. Read passages—but keep them short. Use some of the documentaries, graphic novels, movies, and even animated features that have featured the early Christians.

6. TEACH LIKE THE FATHERS. Put sacraments at the center. Non-Catholics may not understand these mysteries of faith, but when we speak to our own people we should remind them what God has done for them. Through baptism and Eucharist, they have become "partakers of the divine nature"—children of God in the eternal Son of God. St.

Basil said that the moment of baptism extends through the entirety of life. Let's never forget that! Around AD 190, St. Irenaeus said: "Our way of thinking is attuned to the Eucharist, and the Eucharist in turn confirms our way of thinking."[11] For us as for the Fathers, the sacraments are the key to everything.

7. CELEBRATE THE SEASONS. The Church's calendar is the most effective catechism. It tells the story of salvation over and over again, through the beauty of the feasts and fasts. Every day is a new and different chance to teach the Good News, to deliver a bit of doctrine, and to lead people in the ways of prayer.

8. PONDER THE GREAT MARVELS OF THE TRINITY AND THE INCARNATION. Read the Gospels and creeds with the ancient commentaries. See the difference Jesus made in your life and in human history. Don't let these stunning realities become worn coin. Try to catch the mania for doctrine that Gregory of Nyssa found tiresome in his day. We can use a bit of it today! Remember: the ancients were prepared to die or be exiled for small points of the creed. We should love the Faith so well. But we cannot love what we do not know.

9. KEEP YOUR SENSE OF HUMOR. God's in charge, and we already know that the story ends well. As a result, St. Irenaeus could leaven his serious criticism of heresies with hilarious satire. St. Gregory of Nyssa could write a funny and winsome fundraising letter. St. Lawrence the deacon could look up from the gridiron at his executioner and say, "Turn me over. I'm done on this side." Humor can be a sign of hope. And happy Christians proclaim an attractive faith.

10. SEEK THEIR INTERCESSION. The Faith of our Fathers is living still, but so are the men and women who kept that faith. They are saints whose intercession we should seek. They accomplished great things in their allotted time on earth. They can do still more now, for our lives in the Church they love.

So we go to St. Justin, St. Irenaeus, St. Perpetua, St. Hippolytus, St. Cyprian, St. Athanasius, St. Macrina, St. Basil, St. Jerome, St. Augustine . . . and we say: pray for us!

---

11 Quoted in *Catechism of the Catholic Church*, n. 1327.

THE FAMILY ON MISSION

LESSONS FROM THE EARLY CHURCH

YEARS AGO, I CAME ACROSS A CHILDREN'S BOOK that told the history of the early Church in small words and large, brightly colored pictures. The first few centuries were pretty much distilled into a few pages with a simple message, which I'll further summarize here:

The wicked Roman Empire prevailed for a long time, killing Christians by the thousands, till one day the pagan emperor Constantine was crossing a bridge. He looked up into the sky and saw a cross in the clouds and he heard a voice saying, "By this sign, you shall conquer!" So Constantine became a believer, and from that moment on the Roman Empire was a Christian Empire. And we all lived happily ever after. The End.

If only evangelization were that simple! If only God would always make the gospel immediately relevant by raising a huge cross in the sky and thundering a command from above. If only God would transform *our* culture by the miraculous conversion of its most influential leaders.

Ah, if only life were as simple as storybooks.

The truth, however, is more messy than the storybooks let on. Indeed, the Christianizing of the Roman Empire after Constantine was perhaps messier than it had been before, during the centuries of persecution.

Imperial toleration was no cure-all to the Church's woes. Nor was the imperial mandate of Christianity in 380. In fact, many historians believe these circumstances were bad for the Church in the long run.

What did happen in the wake of toleration? The Eastern lands went about the work of Christianizing in a way significantly different from the Western lands; nasty disputes arose regarding the relationship between throne and altar; and it was these controversies, in part, that widened a rift between East and West, which would eventually leave the Eastern peoples vulnerable to the rise of Islam. Ultimately the East-West rift would widen into a schism, tragically dividing the world's Christians.

Well, so much for the storybook ending of a Christian empire. Yet, I believe the truth about the early Christians is more exciting and more instructive than the storybooks convey. It is a story not so much about emperors and armies as about families and how they changed the world.

THE TRUTH IS THAT, BY THE TIME CONSTANTINE legalized the practice of Christianity, the empire was already Christian. Historians believe that by the beginning of the fourth century all the major urban centers of the empire had majority-Christian populations. So Constantine did not so much ensure Christianity's success as acknowledge it. His edict of toleration was overdue recognition that the Church had already won the empire. We were already in the majority, or at least the largest plurality by far. And by the middle of the fourth century there were thirty-three million Christians in an empire of sixty million people.

Now think for a moment about that number: thirty-three million people.

These were not tens of millions of "nominal" Christians or "cultural" Catholics. They could not be. They didn't have that kind of luxury. In the years 293–305, just a decade or so before Constantine's edict, the Church had suffered its most ruthless and systematic persecution under the emperor Diocletian. Historians do not exaggerate when they call it a "holocaust." The practice of the Faith was, in many places, punished by torture and death. To live as a Christian meant, at least, to take on social stigma and humiliation.

What's more, the Christian way itself was characterized by demanding disciplines in the life of prayer and in the moral life. So, no matter how you look at it, to be a Christian was not an easy thing in the year 300 . . . It cost something. Whether or not you were martyred, you had to pay with your life. Thirty-three million Christians were laying their lives on the line every time they attended Mass, and they continued to do so throughout their every day.

Yet the rate of conversion throughout the empire—long before Constantine—was most remarkable. A few years back an eminent sociologist, Rodney Stark, set out to track Church growth in the ancient world. He gathered his findings in a book titled *The Rise of Christianity* (Harper Collins, 1997). Dr. Stark was not a Christian; so he had no vested interest in making us look good.

What he found in his study of the first Christian centuries was an astonishing growth rate. As I mentioned in the opening essay, the Church seems to have grown at a steady pace of 40 percent per decade. Stark holds that most growth came from individual conversions, and not only from the poor, but also from the merchant and upper classes. Using historical data and sociological methods, he argues that the Christian Church grew from about 2 percent of the empire's population in the early third century to slightly over half in the mid-fourth.

Again, Constantine gets no credit for this growth. Much of it happened in the years before he was born. In fact, even though conversions were coerced at various times after the year 380, the Church never again witnessed the kind of growth that took place when conversions were costly.

How and why did this happen? And what can we learn from those early Christians? After all, though the Church today is apparently growing, we've still got a long way to go if we're to catch up with our long-ago ancestors in evangelization.

———————————————

STARK VIVIDLY DESCRIBES THE MISERY of ordinary citizens of the pagan world. Most lived in cramped, smoky tenements with no ventilation or plumbing. Such apartment buildings frequently collapsed or burned.

The cities were horribly crowded. A city like Antioch—where the disciples were first called Christians—had perhaps 200 people per acre, plus livestock (modern Calcutta has only 122 people per acre). Constant immigration meant that the cities were peopled by strangers, with resulting crime and disorder, so that the streets were not safe at night and families were not even safe in their homes.

Life expectancy was around thirty for men and perhaps much lower for women. Hygiene was minimal. Medical care was more dangerous than disease—and disease often left its victims disfigured or dead. The human body was host to countless parasites, and tenements were infested by rats and other pests. For entertainment, people thronged the circuses to see other people mutilated and killed. The corpses of those who died of natural causes were sometimes left to rot in the city's open sewers. It wasn't pretty.

And pagan marriage offered no respite from this misery. Greco-Roman women were usually married off at age eleven or twelve, to a mate who was not of their choosing. Afterward, they suffered in predatory relationships rife with abortion, adultery, and abuse. Infanticide was common, especially for female or "defective" offspring.

Of the six hundred families who show up in the records from ancient Delphi, only six had raised more than one daughter. That's six families out of six hundred! Though many of those six hundred families were quite large families, they had all routinely killed their baby girls. And this was not a geographically isolated trend. A recent archeological dig in the Near East turned up an ancient sewer clogged with the bones of newborns—hundreds of newborns—presumably most of them female.

If fewer girls lived to see the second day from their birth, still more died on their way to adulthood. The shortage of women, then, played further havoc on the population growth of the empire, as well as its economy and its morals.

THAT'S THE WORLD WHERE THE FIRST CHRISTIANS were born, where they grew up and married, and where they raised their families. You might call it a culture of death.

But Christian marriage and childrearing immediately set itself apart. According to Stark, Christian husbands and wives genuinely tried to love one another, as their religion required. Their mutual affection and their openness to fertility led to a higher birth rate, and thus to a still higher growth rate for the early Church.

The early Christians' respect for the dignity of marriage made the Faith enormously attractive to pagan women. So women made up a disproportionate number of the early converts. This situation, in turn, made Christianity enormously attractive to pagan men—who couldn't find many pagan women to marry, but saw young ladies attending the Christian liturgy in great numbers.

We shouldn't dismiss these benefits of Christianity in the natural order. One thing that the rise of Christianity demonstrated is that faithfulness to the one true God is the best way to happiness, not only in heaven, but in the world that God created. One of the fundamental principles of Catholic theology is that grace does not destroy nature, but builds upon it and perfects it.

Christian faith, then as now, makes for happy homes. And, in pagan cultures, then as now, happy homes were very attractive. The evidence seems to indicate that, in the ancient Roman empire, Christian homes provided the Church's primary place of evangelization.

This is a fact we don't find too often in the lives of the saints, which tend to focus on extraordinary events and great miracles. Nor do we find it in Church histories, which tend to focus on the lives of the bishops and the clergy. Yet it is the true story of the Church.

The fire of charity that was tended in the Christian home soon consumed city blocks and then neighborhoods. It wasn't the sort of ecstatic experience we see in the account of the first Pentecost, in the Acts of the Apostles. It was, rather, a quiet and gradual phenomenon.

Let's look at just one example of how this worked.

Epidemics were among the great terrors of life in the ancient world. The physicians in those days knew that the diseases were communicable, but they knew nothing about bacteria or viruses, never mind antibiotics or antisepsis. So, once the diseases hit your hometown, there was really no stopping them. There were several major epidemics during the rise of Christianity, and each of them reduced the empire's population by about one-third.

Yet even in those circumstances the Church grew. In fact, amid simultaneous persecutions and epidemics, the Church grew still more dramatically, especially in proportion to the total population of the empire.

Everyone was dropping like flies, but the Church was growing. How did that happen? Look at what ordinarily occurred when an epidemic hit your hometown. The first people to leave were the doctors. They knew what was coming, and they knew they could do nothing to prevent it.

The next to leave were the pagan priests, because they had the means and the freedom to do so.

Ordinary pagan families were encouraged to abandon their homes when family members contracted the plague. Again, they knew no other way to isolate the disease than to leave the afflicted family member behind to die, perhaps slowly, perhaps quickly.

Yet Christians were duty-bound *not* to abandon the sick. In caring for the sick, Jesus had said that Christians were caring for Christ Himself. So, even though Christians knew no more about medicine than the pagans did, they stayed with their family members, friends, and neighbors who were suffering.

Consider this account of the great epidemic of the year 260, left to us by Bishop Dionysius of Alexandria: "Most of our brother Christians showed unbounded love and loyalty, never sparing themselves and thinking only of one another. Heedless of danger, they took charge of the sick, attending their every need and ministering to them in Christ—and with them departed this life serenely happy; for they were infected by others with the disease, drawing on themselves the sickness of their neighbors and cheerfully accepting their pains . . . Death in this form, the result of great piety and strong faith, seems in every way the equal of martyrdom."[1]

We also possess pagan accounts of that epidemic, and all of them are characterized by despair. Yet the Christians were "serenely happy." Amid all that havoc, Christian charity, which usually began in the family home, had an enormous impact on Church growth. Christians were much more likely to survive epidemics because they cared for one another. Mere comfort care likely cut the Christians' mortality rate by two-thirds, when compared with the pagans'.

What's more, the Christian families cared for their pagan neighbors as well. Thus, the pagans who received Christian care were more likely to survive and, in turn, become Christians themselves. Consequently, in times of epidemic, when population as a whole plummeted, Church growth soared.

And the pagans took notice. The emperor Julian, who despised Christianity and led the charge to re-paganize the empire, still had to grudgingly admire Christian charity: "The impious Galileans support not only their poor, but ours as well. Everyone can see that our poor lack aid from us." [Scholars today

---

1   Quoted in Eusebius, *Church History* 7.22.

speak of the contrast between pagan philanthropy, which was for show, and Christian charity, which was for Christ.]

I can't emphasize enough that this charitable activity was not so much the work of institutions as of families. The family was then, as it is now, the fundamental unit of the Church. Until the third century, most Christians did not have a building they could call their "church." Their worship, like most of the rest of their Christian life, took place in Christian homes. Institutionalized Christian charitable organizations were still years away in the future, to be established during more peaceful times.

In the beginning, charity was, rather, the way of Christian family life.

THIS ROUTINE OF CHARITY did not so much constitute a new culture, replacing the old. Outwardly, little had changed in the neighborhoods inhabited by Christians. The law, the government, the routines of daily life remained as they were—and as they would largely remain, intact, even after Constantine. But inwardly, everything had changed.

We see the means of this transformation, even very early in Christian history. A document of the early second century, the anonymous *Letter to Diognetus* describes the process in profound yet simple terms. The writer points out that Christians are not distinguished from other people by anything external: not their country or language, not their food or clothing, but by what he calls the Christians' "wonderful and striking way of life." "They marry, as do all [others]; they beget children; but they do not commit infanticide. They have a common table, but not a common bed . . . . They obey the prescribed laws, and at the same time surpass the laws by their lives. They love everyone, and are persecuted by everyone . . . To sum it up: As the soul is in the body, so Christians are in the world. The soul is dispersed through all the members of the body, and Christians are scattered through all the cities of the world . . . The invisible soul is guarded by the visible body, and Christians are known indeed to be in the world, but their godliness remains invisible."

Gradually. Invisibly. But inexorably. This is the way that Christian doctrine, hope and charity transformed the Roman Empire—one person at a time. Christianity transformed the way neighbors treated the sick, the way parents treated their children, and the way husbands and wives made love.

That's what really happened to the Roman Empire. The Gospel of Jesus Christ gradually spread, from person to person, from family to family, from home to home, from neighborhood to neighborhood, then to entire provinces. Conversion took place in the smallest increments, one by one, because of homes like yours.

WHEN WE READ ABOUT OUR ANCESTORS in the Faith, their deeds cry out for modern imitation. I'll be so bold as to draw out a few lessons.

1. COME TO SEE YOUR HOME AS A DOMESTIC CHURCH. Modern Christians have a tendency to think of the "church" as their parish buildings. That's a partial truth, but it's not enough. We have to believe that our families are the Church, that our homes are the Church, and that the kingdom of God begins in the place where we hang our hats and eat our meals. We need to imitate the early Christians in seeing our homes as places of worship and fellowship, and as schools of virtue. St. Augustine once addressed a gathering of dads as "my dear fellow bishops."[2] That's the role that parents and grandparents play in the domestic Church.

2. MAKE YOUR DOMESTIC CHURCH A HAVEN OF CHARITY. One of the most striking descriptions of the early Church comes from Tertullian, who wrote: "It is our care of the helpless, our practice of loving kindness that brands us in the eyes of many of our opponents, who say, 'See those Christians, how they love one another.'"[3] This charity has to begin at home. Yet how many Catholics who decry the lack of reverence in their parish church, then go home to desecrate their domestic Churches—by harsh words toward their children or toward their spouses—or by gossip about their neighbors or their coworkers? We will all be called to account for this. Remember the words of Tertullian. They'll know we are Christians—not by the icons on our wall, or the grotto in our front yard—but by the love in our hearts, expressed in our homes.

---

2 St. Augustine, Sermon 94.1.
3 Tertullian, *Apologeticum* 39.7.

3. MAKE YOUR DOMESTIC CHURCH A PLACE OF PRAYER. This doesn't mean that your day has to be dominated by devotions, but you should have some regular, routine family disciplines of prayer. The early Christians saw this as necessary and so observed "stational hours" of prayer throughout the day—and even throughout the night. In the third century, Tertullian described Christian families in North Africa rising in the middle of every night to pray together. Most Christians today don't rise at 3 a.m.; nor am I suggesting we should. There are many ways to pray as a family, and you should seek out the ways that work best for your tribe. The important thing is to do something, start somewhere. Begin with something small and manageable, and then give yourself time to grow into it.

4. MAKE THE MASS THE CENTER OF YOUR FAMILY'S PRAYER LIFE. Families should keep Sunday as a special day, and this takes effort. We're all overscheduled these days, but we should never book our Sunday too solid for the Liturgy—and we should try to get there all together, as a family. Missing Mass should be unthinkable for us, as it was for the early Christians. One of my favorite stories from the early Church is about the Martyrs of Abitina. This was a group of North Africans who lived during the Roman empire's most ruthless persecution. Remember that, for pagans, Sunday was an ordinary workday. So when these families gathered together for Sunday Mass, they were an easy target. In fact, the judge who tried them couldn't believe they would expose themselves so willingly. He asked them why they did, and they told him: "We cannot live without the Mass." They'd rather have died than miss Mass. They chose to die rather than miss Mass. We should be as reluctant to stay home on Sundays and holy days.

5. KNOW THAT, AS A DOMESTIC CHURCH, YOU'RE "ON MISSION." Like the universal Church, you are sent by Christ to bring the Gospel to the world. You are sent outward from your home. You are sent. That's the root meaning of the word apostle, and you and I and all our children are called to be apostles to the world.

Imagine yourself as one of those invisible Christians living in the ancient cities that were rotting with epidemics. What would you do? What would you have your family do? Would you board up the windows and position your shotgun? I don't think so. You would do as your ancestors did and go out and serve your neighbors.

Well, nowadays, medicine exercises a greater degree of control over the ancient plagues. But we should all ask ourselves: What epidemics are consuming the families in our neighborhoods today? What is it that leaves them scarred and barely able to go on in life? How about rejection? Loneliness? Abandonment . . . that constant sense that they're not wanted by someone they dearly love? Perhaps we need to expand our definitions of poverty and epidemic, in order to see the people our families must serve today. There are people on our blocks who are very lonely, elderly and alone, mourning, or otherwise in need. How might our families help? Sometimes it's as simple as making occasional meals, sharing the kids' "artwork" for the neighbors' refrigerators, or opening the door to our homes. One of the Great Fathers of the Western Church, St. Jerome, said:"The eyes of all are turned upon you. Your house is set on a watchtower; your life fixes for others the limits of their self-control."[4] But this statement can't be true unless we open our lives and our homes to others.

6. CULTIVATE THE VIRTUE OF HOPE. Divine grace has unlimited power. It can transform persons; it can and has transformed cultures. We have to believe in miracles. We have to believe that people can change. It's too easy for us to look beyond our backyard and see people who are hopelessly lost, whom the culture has irremediably inoculated against the Gospel. But this is simply not true. Read the agnostic Rodney Stark, and you'll see that miracles do happen: people do change, towns and cities and nations can convert to Christianity. If we have faith the size of a mustard seed, we can do as much with our situation as the ancient Christians did with Greco-Roman culture.

7. FINALLY, LIVE BY THE TEACHINGS OF THE CHURCH. We need to raise our homes up to the standard of Jesus Christ. It's a high standard, but the alternatives today are deadly. The early Christians did not convert the Empire by compromising with the empire's ideas of family life. They did not compromise on divorce, contraception, homosexual activity, abortion, or infanticide. The early Christians hated these sins, even as they passionately loved the sinners who committed these sins—the sinners who lived in their neighborhoods. We, too,

---

4   St. Jerome, Letter 60.14.

need to hate these sins and keep them far from our own homes. But we need also to help other homes, other families to live according to the Church's teachings. We need to evangelize the families who need us.

If we don't, then we can look for ourselves in the parable of the Good Samaritan, where we walk on by with the priest and the levite who ignored the man in the ditch.

But if we do—if we make the effort to evangelize our homes and our neighbors—we'll surely see a new rise of Christianity, and in a couple thousand years children's book can give a true storybook ending to the history of our time.

THE MARTYR'S CUP

LET'S SET OUR TIME MACHINE BACK TWENTY CENTURIES. To July of AD 64, when the world was ruled by Rome, and Rome was ruled by a murderous pervert named Nero. During the tenth year of Nero's reign, a great fire consumed much of the city of Rome. The fire raged out of control for seven days—and then it started again, mysteriously, a day later. Many in Rome knew that Nero had been eager to do some urban redevelopment. He had a plan that included an opulent golden palace for himself. The problem was that so many buildings were standing in his way—many of them teeming wooden tenements housing Rome's poor and working class.

The fire seemed too convenient for Nero's purposes—and his delight in watching the blaze didn't relieve anybody's suspicions. If he didn't exactly fiddle while Rome burned, he at least recited his poems. Nero needed a scapegoat, and an upstart religious cult, Jewish in origin and with foreign associations, served his purposes well. He chose to blame the Christians. Nero was a perverse expert at human torment, and so he had some of these Christians tortured till they were so mad they would confess to any crime. Once they had confessed, he had others arrested.

He must have known, however, that the charges would not hold up. So he condemned them not for arson, or treason, or conspiracy, but for "hatred of humanity."

To amuse the people, he arranged for their execution to be a spectacle, gory entertainment on a grand scale. The Roman historian Tacitus—who had contempt for Christianity, but greater contempt for Nero—describes in gruesome detail the tortures that took place amid a party in Nero's gardens.

> *Mockery of every sort was added to their deaths. Covered with the skins of beasts, they were torn by dogs and perished, or were nailed to crosses, or were doomed to the flames. These served as lamps to light up the night when daylight failed. Nero had thrown open the gardens for the spectacle, and was exhibiting a show in the circus, while he mingled with the people in the dress of a charioteer or drove about in a chariot. Hence, even for criminals who deserved extreme and exemplary punishment there arose a feeling of compassion; for it was not, as it seemed, for the public good, but to glut one man's cruelty, that they were being punished.[1]*

That is all we know about the first Roman martyrs. We know none of their names. The pagan Tacitus doesn't tell us why they were willing to die this way rather than renounce their faith. Yet this should be an important question for us to consider. Why did the martyrs do this? What prepared them to face death so bravely? To what exactly did they bear witness with their death?

Let us begin with the witness we know best and ask ourselves: How can we spot a Christian today? What are the unmistakable signs that tell us we're with a fellow believer?

In the first generation of the Church, there were several unmistakable signs. St. Luke tells us that the first Christians, one and all, "devoted themselves to the teaching of the apostles and to the communion (*koinonia*), to the breaking of the bread and to the prayers" (Acts 2:42). The teaching of the apostles, the communion, the breaking of the bread, and the prayers.

This is a precious snapshot, because we do not know as much about those first Christians as we would like to know. They were a small group, not especially wealthy, without social or political status, and often operating underground. What's more, over the next two hundred and fifty years,

---

1 Tacitus, *Annals* 15.44.

imperial and local governments tried fairly regularly to wipe out all traces of Christianity—destroying not only the Christians' bodies, but their books and their possessions as well. So what we have left are the handful of documents that survived—mostly sermons, letters, and liturgies—as well as a few other scraps of parchment or painted wood, and the shards of pottery that the desert sands have preserved for us.

Yet what we see in those surviving documents and what we find in the archeological digs confirm all that we learn in the Acts of the Apostles: The first Christians "devoted themselves to the apostolic teaching, to the communion, and to the breaking of the bread and the prayers." That is, they devoted themselves to the Mass, for the Mass is where all those actions come together.

Our first Christian ancestors devoted themselves to the Eucharist, and that is perhaps the most important way they showed themselves to be Christians. No Christian practice is so well attested from those early years. No doctrine is so systematically worked out as the doctrine of the Eucharist.

Christianity spread rapidly through the Roman Empire, and that meant that the Mass was celebrated everywhere. And the ubiquity of the Mass was itself a favorite theme of the earliest Church fathers. St. Justin Martyr commented that, by his lifetime, by the year 150, there was "not one single race of men . . . among whom prayers and Eucharist are not offered through the name of the crucified Jesus."[2]

The ancient Fathers commonly applied the Old Testament prophecy of Malachi to the liturgy: "from the rising of the sun to its setting my name is great among the nations, and in every place incense is offered to my name, and a pure offering." Those lines found their way into many Eucharistic prayers, where they remain even to this day. ("so that from east to west a perfect offering may be made to the glory of your name.")

As the Church moved outward from Jerusalem, this is what believers did. They offered the Mass. The early histories tell us that the first thing the Apostle Jude did when he established the Church in the city of Edessa was to ordain priests and to teach them to celebrate the Mass.

The Mass is what the early Church was about. Everything that was good in Christian life flowed naturally and supernaturally from that one great Eucharistic reality: from the Christians' sacramental experience of fellowship

---

2   St. Justin Martyr, *Dialogue with Trypho* 41.

and communion, of the teaching of the apostles, of the breaking of the bread, and of the prayers.

But there was another dominant reality in the ancient Church. It is something that appears just as often in the archeological record and in the paper trail of the early Christians. That something is martyrdom. Persecution.

Martyrdom occupied the attention of the first Christians because it was always a real possibility. Shortly after Christianity arrived in the city of Rome, the emperor Nero discovered that Christians could provide an almost unlimited supply of victims for his circus spectacles. The emperors needed to keep the people amused, and one way to do so was by giving them spectacularly violent and bloody entertainments.

So the Christians were doused with pitch and set on fire, or sent into the ring to battle hungry wild animals or armed gladiators. It was all in a day's fun in ancient Rome. Over time, Nero's perverted whims settled into laws and legal precedents, as later emperors issued further rulings on the Christian problem. Outside the law, mob violence against Christians was fairly common and rarely punished.

The Christians applied a certain term to their co-religionists who were made victims of persecution. They called them "martyrs"—*martures*—which means, literally, witnesses in a court of law. And to the martyrs they accorded a reverence matched only by their reverence for the Eucharist.

In fact, the early Christians used the same language to describe martyrdom as they used to describe the Eucharist. We see this in the New Testament Book of Revelation, when John describes his vision of heaven. There, he saw "under the altar the souls of those who had been slain for the word of God and for the witness they had borne." There, *under the altar of sacrifice*, were the martyrs, the witnesses.

That image brings it all together. For, in those first generations of the Church, the most common phrase used to describe the Mass was "the sacrifice." Both the *Didache* and St. Ignatius refer to it as "*the* sacrifice." And yet martyrdom, too, was *the sacrifice*.

And so, in AD 107, when Ignatius described his own impending execution, he imagined it in Eucharistic terms. He said he was like the wine at the offertory. He wrote to the Romans: "Grant me nothing more than that I be poured out to God, while an altar is still ready."[3] Later in the same letter he wrote: "Let me be food for the wild beasts, through whom I can reach God.

---

3   St. Ignatius of Antioch, *Letter to the Romans* 4.

I am God's wheat, ground fine by the lion's teeth to be made purest bread for Christ." Ignatius is bread, and he is wine; his martyrdom is a sacrifice. It's a eucharist.

Ignatius's good friend Polycarp also died a martyr's death. Polycarp was bishop of Smyrna, and had been converted by the Apostle John himself. Polycarp's secretary wrote a detailed account of the bishop's martyrdom, and he described it, once again, as a kind of eucharist. Polycarp's final words are a long prayer of thanksgiving that echoes the great Eucharistic prayers of the ancient world and today. It includes an invocation of the Holy Spirit, a doxology of the Trinity, and a great Amen at the end.[4]

When the flames reached the body of the old bishop, his secretary tells us that the pyre gave off not the odor of burning flesh but the aroma of baking bread. In yet another martyrdom, then, we find a pure offering of bread —a eucharist.

The Eucharistic images in Ignatius and Polycarp echo again in the future writings and histories of the martyrs. Even in the court transcripts, presumably taken down by pagan Romans, the Christians reply to the charges against them with lines from the liturgy. They lift up their hearts. And when they are sentenced, they say *Deo gratias*—thanks be to God.

The story of the martyr Pionius proceeds in the words, verbatim, of the Eucharistic prayer: "and looking up to heaven he gave thanks to God."[5] The Greek word for "thanks" there is *eucharistesas*. So we might read it as, "Looking up to heaven, he offered the Eucharist to God," even as the flames consumed him. In a similar way, the priest Irenaeus cried out, in the midst of torture, "With my endurance I am even now offering sacrifice to my God to whom I have always offered sacrifice."[6]

So pervasive is this Eucharistic language in the early Church's written records that one of the great scholars of early Christianity, Robin Darling Young of Notre Dame, has spoken of the ancient Church as having two liturgies: the *private* liturgy of the Mass and the *public* liturgy of martyrdom.[7]

---

4   *Martyrdom of Polycarp* 15.
5   *Acts of Pionius* 21.
6   *The Martyrdom of St. Irenaeus, Bishop of Sirmium.*
7   See Robin Darling Young, *In Procession Before the World: Martyrdom as Public Liturgy in Early Christianity* (Milwaukee: Marquette University Press, 2001). See also Finbarr G. Clancy, S.J., "Imitating the Mysteries That You Celebrate: Martyrdom and Eucharist in the Early Patristic Period," in *The Great Persecution: The Proceedings of the Fifth Patristic Conference*, Maynooth, 2003 (Dublin: Four Courts, 2009), 106f.

But what is it about martyrdom that makes it like the Mass? Well, what has Jesus done in the Mass? He has given Himself to us, and He has held nothing back. He gives us His Body, Blood, Soul, and Divinity. He gives Himself to us as food. And that's love: the total gift of self. That is the very love the martyrs wanted to imitate. Jesus had given Himself entirely for them. They wanted to give themselves entirely for Him—everything they had, holding nothing back. If Jesus would become bread for them, they would allow the lions to make them finest wheat for Jesus.

So: Martyrdom was a total gift of self. The Eucharist was a total gift of self. In the Eucharist, Jesus gave Himself to us. In martyrdom, we give ourselves back to Him.

But there's a problem here. We know that very few of the ancient Christians died for the Faith. What about the rest? What was their gift? How did they live the Eucharist?

Well, not long after Christianity was legalized by the Emperor Constantine, St. Jerome noted that some believers were already growing nostalgic for the good old days of the martyrs. But Jerome stopped such fantasies in their tracks. He told his congregation, "Let's not think that there is martyrdom only in the shedding of blood. There is always martyrdom."[8]

There is always martyrdom. For most of the early Christians, the martyrdom came not with lions or fire or the rack or the sword. It came not at the hands of a mob or a gladiator. For most of the early Christians, "martyrdom" consisted in a daily dying to self in imitation of Jesus Christ.

Jesus told them: "If anyone would come after me, let him deny himself . . . daily." So the Christians denied themselves, in imitation of Jesus. What did this mean, in practical terms? It meant that they would never eat lavishly as long as others were going hungry. They would never keep an opulent wardrobe while others dressed in rags. They would never hold back their *testimony to the Faith* as long as *any* of their neighbors were living in sin or in ignorance of the love of Jesus Christ.

Whatever they had, those Christians gave. They gave of themselves—just as the martyrs gave themselves in the arena—just as Jesus Christ gave Himself on the Cross—and just as Jesus Christ gave Himself in the Eucharist.

In Christ, these Christians had come into a Holy Communion. In baptism, they were baptized into His death, into Christ's own martyrdom.

---

8   St. Jerome, *De Persecutione Christianorum*, quoted in Boniface Ramsey, *Beginning to Read the Fathers* (Mahwah, NJ: Paulist, 1985), 133.

In the Mass they became one with Him in the deepest, and closest, and most intimate bond possible. They were closer to Jesus than they were to their best friends, closer to Him than they were to their spouses. They were closer to Jesus than they were to their own parents or their own children. He Himself had promised them that they would live in Him, and He would live in them.

This was, and is, the deepest truth of the Faith. In Jesus Christ we live as sons and daughters of the eternal Father—we share His own divine life. In Jesus Christ we can call God our Father because God is eternally His Father. In the New Testament, St. Peter puts our Holy Communion in the most powerful terms: We have "become partakers of the divine nature" (2 Pet. 1–4).

And what is that nature? How does God live in eternity? What is the Trinity for us, besides a theological abstraction and a mathematical enigma?

John said it all: God is Love. God is—as my friend Scott Hahn puts it— self-giving, life-giving love. From all eternity, God the Father pours Himself out in love for the Son. He holds nothing back. The Son returns that love to the Father with everything He has. He holds nothing back. And the love that they share is the Holy Spirit.

This is the life the martyrs knew even at the moment of their death— *especially* at the moment of their death. But they themselves had been caught up into that life so long before and so many times. They themselves had been caught up into the life-giving love of Jesus Christ—the life-giving love of the Blessed Trinity—whenever they had gone to Mass. Whenever they had received Holy Communion. Whenever they had joined with their brothers and sisters for the teaching of the apostles and the communion, the breaking of the bread and the prayers.

Jesus gave Himself entirely to them, and they gave themselves in return. At every Eucharist, He gives Himself entirely to us, and we give ourselves entirely in return. We say Amen—So be it!—I accept. And when we do that, we consent to the communion.

We need to know what we're doing when we say "Amen." The life of Christ is more than a warm, fuzzy feeling that I'm OK and you're OK and everything will work out fine. When we say Amen to the Body of Christ we're accepting the cross of Christ as our own. We're accepting our own martyrdom.

And in the words of Garrison Keillor: If you don't want to go to Minneapolis, what are you doing on the train?

There is *always* martyrdom. St. Paul had signaled this in his Letter to the Romans, where he wrote: "I appeal to you therefore, brethren, by the mercies of God, to present your bodies as a living sacrifice, holy and acceptable to God, which is your spiritual worship" (Rom. 12:1). Surely Paul's words reached many future martyrs in Rome, where he himself would one day die by beheading.

But his words reached many others as well, men and women whose sacrifice would be something quiet and hidden and noticed only by God. The same St. Paul referred to our bodies as "temples of the Holy Spirit." Let's never forget that in the ancient world temples were not mere shrines; they were places of sacrifice.

And so are we. Our bodies are places of sacrifice, and our lives are the offering on the altar. We ourselves are the Mass in motion. A Mass mobilization.

Our everyday life should be a voluntary sacrifice, voluntary self-giving, voluntary witness, voluntary martyrdom. Listen to the Church's traditional language of penance and reparation, mortification, fasting, pilgrimage, and almsgiving. It's all about self-possession, self-denial, self-mastery. And all that is great. It's good to be disciplined, and self-denial is a means to achieving discipline. But discipline, too, is a means and not an end in itself. Why do we want to possess ourselves?

Jesus shows us why. We possess ourselves in order to give ourselves away— just like Jesus, just like the martyrs. Only then can we become truly ourselves. For we are made in God's image, and God is life-giving love, whose human life was a self-giving sacrifice. The Mass is that sacrifice, and all our lives must be placed upon the altar, all our lives must be taken up into the Eucharist—all the hours we spend at our desks or workstations, in our kitchens or classrooms.

Remember the question I asked earlier: How can we spot a Christian today? The same way we could have spotted them on the streets of first-century Rome or Jerusalem: by their Eucharistic lives. When we give ourselves without holding back, we are living like the early Christians. We are living like the martyrs. We are living like the Most Blessed Trinity in heaven. We are living that famous teaching of St. Irenaeus of Lyons: "Our way of thinking is attuned to the Eucharist, and the Eucharist in turn confirms our way of thinking."[9]

What does this Eucharistic life look like in the day-to-day? You've seen it yourself. It looks like a mother staying up all night with a sick child—or grandparents up late with the child so that their daughter can get some sleep.

---

9   St. Irenaeus of Lyons, *Against the Heresies* 3.3.2.

It looks like a husband working hard, working long hours at a task he doesn't particularly enjoy, so that his family can know a better life. It looks like a family keeping vigil by a deathbed. It looks like the dying man who musters a smile for the sake of his loved ones, even though he doesn't feel like smiling.

As Jerome said: "Let's not think that there is martyrdom only in the shedding of blood. There is *always* martyrdom." And it's always our vocation.

And this martyrdom, too—even when it is just the martyrdom of a kindly smile—is a public witness. Our dutiful dedication to our work and our families should be an outward sign of a profound inner sacrifice, a Christ-like gift of ourselves. What we do should be a sacrament of who we are. There's a beautiful passage in the Old Testament that speaks of such witness, again in sacrificial terms:

> *But the souls of the righteous are in the hand of God,*
> *and no torment will ever touch them . . .*
> *because God tested them and found them worthy of himself;*
> *like gold in the furnace he tried them,*
> *and like a sacrificial burnt offering he accepted them.*
> *In the time of their visitation they will shine forth,*
> *and will run like sparks through the stubble. (Wis. 3:1–7)*

That's the total gift of self. It's what the early Christians knew. And it's what we must all come to know for ourselves, if we want to become ourselves— if we want to become what God made us to be. There's no other way to be happy. It's all there in the Mass of the early Christians, and in the Eucharist we attend on Sunday, the Eucharist we're called to live every day of our lives.

ECUMENISM

IN THE NICK OF TIME

THERE'S A CERTAIN KIND OF CATHOLIC—usually male, but not always—who likes nothing more than a good inter-Christian tussle. Blogger Mark Shea once wrote that if these guys weren't so devout, they'd be hanging around bars picking fights. Their model, among the ancient Christians, is no doubt St. Nicholas of Myra, who reportedly punched the heretic Arius in the nose at the Council of Nicea in AD 325. (Yes, I mean Santa Claus. And the story goes that a profusion of blood came forth from Arius. "Happy holidays, infidel.")

Now, don't get me wrong: I have a great devotion to St. Nicholas. In fact, he's one of the handful of saints whose intercession I invoke every day of my life. But his was not the only way the Church fathers approached ecumenism.

Consider Pope Zephyrinus, in the second century. In the midst of fierce persecution from imperial Rome, the poor guy also had to face heresies and moral lapses within the Church. The situation grew to scandal proportions, but he endured it patiently. In fact, some rigorists thought he was far *too* patient with heretics and sinners. The rigorists' own holy impatience soon turned ugly—and unholy—as they declared the pope *anathema* and the worldwide Church his "sect." Meanwhile, they dubbed their own little congregation "the Catholic Church." They elected history's first antipope—a man who, in his rather extreme aggression, tended to over-correct the errors of the heretics and fall into the heresies on the opposite side of the tracks.

Pope St. Zephyrinus remained steady and orthodox. He knew when to pull his punches, just as St. Nicholas allegedly knew when to throw them. As someone once said, there is "a time to rend, and a time to sew; a time to keep silence, and a time to speak; a time to love, and a time to hate; a time for war, and a time for peace" (Eccles. 3:7–8).

Still today, it's easy for armchair pontiffs to grumble about the perceived weaknesses of the real popes. It's the real ones who have the thankless job of discerning the seasons of the carrot and the seasons of the stick. We should avoid grumbling and learn patience from history.

The Church of the Fathers suffered many divisions—schisms, heresies, and outright apostasies. There were certainly occasions for excommunication, but prayer for unity was always in season. And we can be sure that all those prayers of the Fathers will one day be answered. Many, in fact, *were* answered, in short order and rather definitively, as the ancient heresies exhausted themselves. Sometimes it took centuries, but the errors of the Montanists, Marcionites, Arians, Apollinarians, and Monothelites all went the way of the wooly mammoth.

One of the most painful divisions in Christian antiquity was the schism that rent the Persian East from the Byzantine and Roman West. It happened with the Nestorian schism in the fifth century, when a serious doctrinal dispute gained further momentum from cultural and political tensions. The division has lasted now for a millennium and a half.

There are Catholics, no doubt, who would consider this division a "cold case," meriting no further attention. But Pope John Paul II chose to give it his closest attention. He encouraged the dialogue. And in 1994, he signed a "Common Christological Declaration" with Patriarch Mar Dinkha IV of the Church of the East, essentially resolving "the main dogmatic problem between the Catholic Church and the Assyrian Church." In 2001, the Pontifical Council for Promoting Christian Unity went a step further and approved the sharing of Communion between the (Catholic) Chaldean Church and the (so-called Nestorian) Assyrian Church of the East.

We should marvel that reconciliation should proceed so swiftly after a millennium and a half of alienation. We should marvel at the stunning fact of intercommunion. And, again, we should learn from history: ecumenism proceeds best on God's schedule, not ours.

We should pray for unity. And we should rest assured, as the Fathers did, that our prayer will be answered; for it is the prayer of Jesus (see Jn. 17:11).

Oh, and it's probably best if we hold our punches. That pugilistic Santa Claus story is almost unique in ancient Church history, and scholars tell us it's of dubious origin anyway.

AH, YOUTH

WHEN THE CHURCH WAS YOUNG

THE CHURCH FATHERS HAD A DISTINCTIVE APPROACH to youth ministry. I discovered it in the course of an afternoon's research.

Scouring the *Patrologia Latina* and *Patrologia Graeca*, I found nothing to suggest that Ambrose had ever led teens on ski trips to the nearby Alps. Digging through the Eastern Fathers, I came up even drier—no junior-high dances—not even a pizza party in either Antioch or Alexandria. In fact, in all the documentary evidence from all the ancient patriarchates of the East and the West, there's not a single bulletin announcement for a single parish youth group.

Yet the Fathers had enormous success in youth and young-adult ministry. Many of the early martyrs were teens, as were many of the Christians who took to the desert for the solitary life. There's ample evidence that a disproportionate number of conversions, too, came from the young and youngish age groups.

How did the Fathers do it?

They made wild promises.

They promised young people great things, like persecution, lower social status, public ridicule, severely limited employment opportunities, frequent fasting, a high risk of jail and torture, and maybe, just maybe, an early, violent death at the hands of their pagan rulers.

The Fathers looked young people in the eye and called them to live purely in the midst of a pornographic culture. They looked at some young men and women and boldly told them they had a calling to virginity. And it worked. Even the pagans noticed how well it worked.

The brightest young man in the empire's brightest city—a teenager named Origen of Alexandria—promised himself entirely to God in virginity. And, as he watched his father taken away to be killed, Origen would have gone along himself, turned himself in, if his mother hadn't hidden all his clothes...

I searched volumes on the ancient liturgy, and I was unable to find a scrap of a Mass we'd call "relevant" today. There were no special Youth Masses. Yet there was an overwhelming Eucharistic faith among the young people of the Church.

Tarcisius was a boy of third-century Rome. His virtue and devotion were so strong that the clergy trusted him to bring the Blessed Sacrament to the sick. Once, while carrying a pyx, he was recognized and set upon by a pagan mob. They flung themselves upon him, trying to pry the pyx from his hands, wanting more than anything to profane the Sacrament. Tarcisius' biographer, the fourth-century Pope Damasus, compared them to a pack of rabid dogs. Tarcisius "preferred to give up his life rather than yield up the Body of Christ."

Even at such an early age, Tarcisius was aware of the stakes. Jesus had died for love of Tarcisius. Tarcisius did not hesitate to die for love of Jesus.

What made the Church attractive in the third century can make it just as attractive in the twenty-first. In the ancient world and in ours, young people want a challenge. They want to love with their whole being. They're willing to do things the hard way—if people they respect make the big demands. These are distinguishing marks of youth. You don't find too many middle-aged men petitioning the Marines for a long stay at Parris Island. It's young men who beg for that kind of rigor.

The spiritual writer Father John Hugo told a cautionary tale, not from the ancient Church, but from the German Church of the early twentieth century. Youth leaders faced a country depressed and dejected from its defeat in World War I. Teens seemed aimless, with little hope for professional opportunity and no clear sense of patriotism or other ideals.

The German clergy made a conscious effort, then, to accentuate the positive. They decided to accommodate the country's weakness, avoid mentioning sacrifice, and downplay the cross and other "negative" elements of Christianity. They were big on nature hikes.

At the same time, there arose a man who called upon those same youth to give up everything for the sake of their country. "He put them in uniforms, housed them in barracks—in short, he demanded that they live a hard and laborious life." This man, Adolf Hitler, won the hearts of the youth. Because no young man or woman really wants to give his life away cheaply.

Tarcisius knew better. So do the kids in your parish.

NEWMAN'S CONVERSION

FROM "THE FATHERS OF THE CHURCH" TO "THE CHURCH OF THE FATHERS"

FOR A BRIEF MOMENT IN SEPTEMBER 2010, John Henry Newman caught the attention of the world. As Pope Benedict XVI declared him "blessed," during an apostolic visit to England, Newman's conversion story was once again newsworthy, as it had been a century and a half before.

At the heart of Newman's conversion was his study of the early Christians, the Fathers of the Church. As an Anglican clergyman, he believed that they held the answer to his denomination's perennial problem—its fragmentation in doctrinal and practical matters. Newman sought a purer reflection upon Scripture in the writings of the Fathers, an interpretation untainted by modern politics and controversies. Yet his methods were—and remain— particularly appealing to modern readers.

Newman read the Fathers deeply, and not merely to extract theoretical propositions. He wanted to enter their world—to "see" divine worship as they saw it, to experience the prayers as they prayed them, to insert himself into the drama of the ancient arguments. He immersed himself in the works of the Fathers, so that he could recount their stories in his brief "Historical Sketches," in his book-length studies and, later, in one of his novels.

After decades of such labors, he concluded that, "of all existing systems, the present communion of Rome is the nearest approximation in fact to the Church of the Fathers . . . Did St. Athanasius or St. Ambrose come suddenly to life, it cannot be doubted what communion he would take to be his own."[1]

An interesting thing had happened. His study of the Fathers of the Church had caused him to desire *The Church of the Fathers* (yet another of his book titles). He wanted to place himself in real communion with the ancients, with Athanasius and Ambrose. A notional or theoretical connection wasn't enough, and could never be. He wanted to move out of the shadows of hypothetical churches, based on a selective reading of the Church fathers, and into the reality of the Fathers' Church.

In declaring Newman blessed, Pope Benedict has held up his life as worthy of imitation. And, in the matter of encountering the Fathers, it should hardly be a burden.

Like Newman and his contemporaries, so many people today hold a lively curiosity about Christian origins. Like Newman, many ordinary Christians would like to move beyond the rather petty preoccupations of today's tenure-track historians and documentarians (gender and conflict, conflict and gender). They would like to find their own imaginative entry into the world of the Fathers, the Church of the Fathers. They would like "Historical Sketches" that were vivid enough to see with an attentive mind's eye.

And what would we see as we pored over the works of the Fathers? What would we see as we gazed through the window provided by archeology of early Christian sites?

We would see many familiar sights and sounds, fragrances and gestures.

▷ A CHURCH GATHERED AROUND THE EUCHARIST. This emerges most vividly, not only in the Scriptures, but in the generation immediately after that of the Apostles, the generation of the so-called Apostolic Fathers. The document called "The Didache" (c. AD 48) includes the earliest Eucharistic prayers. Clement of Rome (c. AD 67) sets out the different roles of clergy and laity as they come together for Mass. Ignatius of Antioch (c. AD 107) describes the Eucharist as "the flesh of Christ" and treats the Sacrament as the principle of the

---

1   Blessed John Henry Newman, *An Essay on the Development of Christian Doctrine* (London: James Toovey, 1845), 138.

Church's unity. By the time we get to Justin Martyr (c. AD 155) we find a full description of the Roman Mass that's recognizable enough to be reproduced verbatim in the Church's catechism today.

▷ A CHURCH THAT PRACTICES SACRAMENTAL CONFESSION. The Fathers argued amongst themselves about whether the Church should be strict or lenient in dispensing penance—but none of them denied that this was the right and role of the Church and her clergy. The Fathers heard confessions. They pronounced absolution.

▷ A CHURCH WHOSE MEMBERS MAKE THE SIGN OF THE CROSS. At the end of the second century, Tertullian spoke of the Sign as if it were the hallmark of ordinary, everyday Christian living. Among his wife's beautiful qualities he mentioned the way she made the Sign of the Cross at night.

▷ A CHURCH WHOSE MEMBERS BLESS THEMSELVES WITH HOLY WATER. The "prayerbook" of St. Serapion of Egypt (fourth century) includes a blessing for holy water. Eusebius (late third century) describes the familiar font at the entrance to a Church.

▷ A CHURCH WITH AN ESTABLISHED, SACRAMENTAL HIERARCHY. St. Ignatius of Antioch shows us that, as the first century turned over to the second, the order of the Church was already well established everywhere. As he wrote letters to various churches, he assumed that each church was governed by bishops, presbyters, and deacons. He didn't explain this. He didn't argue for it. He just assumed it. At the turn of the next century, Clement of Alexandria also presented this order as traditional—an imitation of the hierarchy of angels in heaven.

▷ A CHURCH THAT VENERATES THE SAINTS. This shows up in the graffiti on the walls of the Roman catacombs. It shows up in the art of the cemeteries of the Fayoum in Egypt. It shows up in many lamps and medals and signet rings. St. John Chrysostom and St. Augustine wrote numerous homilies on the lives of the saints. The most ancient liturgies invoke their intercession. This is especially true of the Virgin Mary, whose prayers are included in canonical collections by the early third century.

▷ A CHURCH THAT PRAYS FOR THE DEAD. In the 100s, devotional literature describes votive Masses celebrated at gravesides. The earliest tombstones in Christian Rome ask prayers for the deceased. The prison diary of St. Perpetua (North Africa, early third century) includes a vision of purgatory—whose existence is explained theologically by Origen (Egypt, third century). At the end of the second century, Tertullian describes prayer for the dead as already an ancient practice!

▷ A CHURCH WITH A DISTINCTIVE SEXUAL ETHIC AND CLEAR IDEAS ABOUT MARRIAGE AND FAMILY. The early Christians stood almost alone in their refusal to acknowledge divorce, to engage in homosexual activity, to procure or practice abortion, or to use contraception. Their view of sex as sacred made them a laughingstock in the pagan world, where sex was cheap and degrading, and people were, accordingly, miserable.

That's just a glimpse of the early Church, but it's enough to make it recognizable as Catholic. Nor did the Fathers see their life as in any way opposed to Scripture. Scripture and Tradition coexisted in harmony because they had been received from the same Apostles. The Bible's New Testament shows us the Apostles writing letters, yes, but also observing rites, customs, and disciplines.

Moreover, the Church of the Apostles pre-existed the New Testament and shows us that authority, for Christians, does not rest simply in the Scriptures. "First of all you must understand this, that no prophecy of scripture is a matter of one's own interpretation" (2 Pet. 1:20). For the Fathers, interpretation belonged to the Church and her bishops. Polycarp of Smyrna took that lesson well from his master, the Apostle John. In the middle of the second century, he wrote: "Whoever distorts the oracles of the Lord according to his own perverse inclinations . . . is the first-born of Satan."[2] Polycarp's great disciple, Irenaeus of Lyons, made that one of the foundational principles of his multi-volume work, "Against the Heresies."

Newman knew that, standing apart from the Catholic Church, he was standing not with the Church of the Fathers, but rather with the heretics. So he came home, and his way—the Way of the Fathers—has been traversed by many non-Catholics since then.

It's a good bet that many more will follow, rather soon.

As Newman said, "it cannot be doubted" which Christian body the ancient Church most resembles. When we look to the "roots of the Faith," we see today what Newman saw and acknowledged—though it made him

---

2 Reported in St. Irenaeus, *Against the Heresies* 3.3.4.

an uneasy Protestant. If we continue our prayerful study, we hope to follow him further still—to the fullness of faith, blessedness of life, and happiness of heaven.

THE TIME CAPSULE

A COMMONPLACE NOTION OF THE CATHOLIC FAITH is that revelation closed with the death of the last apostle. To us, it's commonplace. But to the early Christians, it was a most urgent matter.

As the apostles went to their martyrdom, one by one, the flock they left behind saw vanishing the only eyewitnesses to Jesus' teaching—the only guarantors of Christian orthodoxy.

It was then, in the first century, that the Christian community produced what we might call its first "catechism," a book that bears the title *The Teaching of the Lord to the Gentiles Through the Twelve Apostles*—or, in Greek, simply the *Didache*, the "teaching."

The *Didache* is actually more than a catechism. It's a "church order" (to use the technical term), a book that combines doctrinal summary with liturgical instruction and a little bit of moral exhortation. It's like a missal, a confessor's manual, and a catechism rolled into one. We possess several church orders from Christian antiquity, but the *Didache* is almost certainly the oldest, and most of the later ones depend upon the *Didache*.

How old is the *Didache*? Most scholars place its composition between AD 60 and 110. However, one of the top scholars alive, Enrico Mazza, argues very persuasively that the liturgical portions of the document were composed no later than AD 48. If he's correct, that means that our oldest liturgical texts pre-date most of the books of the New Testament.

The *Didache*, which was rediscovered at the end of the 19th century, reads like a time capsule from the apostolic generation.

Twenty-first century Christians tend to romanticize those founding years of the Church as a golden age of unity, when believers absorbed sound doctrine by osmosis, and when Christians couldn't help but love one another, and bless their persecutors, and feed the poor.

But that's not how it was. Early on, the Church faced serious threats from self-proclaimed Christians who denied, for example, that the eternal Word truly became flesh (see 1 Jn. 4:2 and 2 Jn. 1:7). They also denied the reality of the Eucharist and the necessity of the Church. Quite early in the game, there were even some teachers who held that revelation was a private affair between God and the individual believer. They spun wildly creative religious systems (see 1 Tim. 1:4) and gave a green-light to unbridled lust (see Jude 7). To legitimize their "revelations," such heretics often attributed oracles to the apostles (see Gal. 1:7 and 2 Thess. 2:2).

Amid this confusion came order and orthodoxy in the *Didache*. It is, perhaps, the earliest ancestor of today's *Catechism of the Catholic Church*. And, indeed, the new *Catechism* quotes that first one several times. (See numbers 1696 on the "two ways," 2271 on abortion, 2760 and 2767 on the Our Father, 1331 on the Eucharist, and 1403 on the Maranatha.)

Many scholars believe that the *Didache* was compiled from various oral and written sources in Antioch of Syria, the place where the disciples of Jesus were first called Christians (Acts 11:26).

Tradition holds that St. Peter, the first pope, was the founding bishop of Antioch, and one of the earliest titles given to the *Didache* was "The Judgments of Peter."

The document is small, just sixteen brief chapters, but it manages to cover a wide area, from morals to sacraments, from prophecy to liturgy. The opening sections (chapters 1–7) offer an exposition of Christian life, emphasizing Christianity's distinctiveness from pagan ways.

"Two ways there are, one of life and one of death, and there is a great difference between the two ways," the *Didache* begins. "Now the way of life is this: first, love the God who made you; secondly, love your neighbor as yourself."

What follows, then, is a remarkable synopsis of Jesus' teachings in a series of quotations and paraphrases. Strung together in a continuous narrative are the Golden Rule, excerpts from the Sermon on the Mount, and commentary on the Ten Commandments. Then, in contrast, the way of death appears as a catalog of vices.

The second section (chapters 7–9) is stunning in its picture of Catholic life. It begins with detailed instructions on baptism: the Sacrament should be conferred in running water, it says, and by immersion, if possible. But the *Didache* also makes allowance for our current custom of pouring water over the head of the candidate.

The early Church, like the Church in recent years, fasted on Fridays, but also on Wednesdays. The traditional day for celebration of the Eucharist was Sunday. Christians, counsels the *Didache*, should pray the Our Father three times every day.

Three chapters of the *Didache* deal specifically with the liturgy, advising the faithful how to prepare and conduct themselves, and prescribing prayers for the clergy. The unknown author makes clear that, even at this early date, the Church reserved Holy Communion only for those who were baptized and free of any grave sin. "Let no one eat or drink of your Eucharist unless they have been baptized . . . If any one is holy, let him come; if any one is not so, let him repent." Repentance normally involved confession of one's sins: "receive the Eucharist after having confessed your transgressions, that your sacrifice may be pure."

The Eucharistic Prayer of the *Didache* emphasizes the Mass's power to unify the Church: "We thank you, our Father, for the life and knowledge which you made known to us through Jesus your servant; to you be the glory forever. Even as this broken bread was scattered over the hills, and was gathered together and became one, so let your Church be gathered together from the ends of the earth into your kingdom; for yours is the glory and the power through Jesus Christ for ever."

After Communion, those early Christians were urged to give thanks in this way: "We thank you, holy Father, for your holy name which you caused to dwell in our hearts, and for the knowledge and faith and immortality, which you made known to us through Jesus your servant; to you be the glory forever. Almighty Master, You created all things for your name's sake; You gave food and drink to men for enjoyment, that they might give thanks to you; but to us you freely gave spiritual food and drink and life eternal through Your servant. Before all things we thank you that you are mighty; to you be the glory forever. Remember, Lord, your Church, to deliver it from all evil and to make it perfect in your love, and gather it from the four winds, sanctified for your kingdom which you have prepared for it; for yours is the power and the glory forever. Let grace come, and let this world pass away. Hosanna to the God (Son) of David! If any one is holy, let him come; if any one is not so, let him repent. *Maranatha.* Amen."

The text appears to be published as canonical, "official" rites, but with room for inspired charismatic expression: "Permit the prophets to give thanks as much as they desire."

The modern Catholic will see much that is familiar in the *Didache* and little that is alien to our experience. Perhaps the most striking differences are in attitude. The first Christians lived with a strong sense of the imminence of Jesus' return—as he is really present in the Eucharist. "Let grace come, and let this world pass away . . . *Maranatha.*" Some scholars believe that *Maranatha,* meaning "Come, Lord!" was the primitive Church's prayer of consecration in the liturgy.

The *Didache* shows that, in structure, the early Church resembled the modern in many ways, with bishops and deacons set apart for ministry to the rest of the community. Those who held teaching offices taught with authority, and we can see that their teaching has remained constantly with the Church. Thus the *Didache* shows that from the beginning the apostles condemned abortion: "You shall not kill the embryo by abortion, and shall not cause the newborn to perish."

Since the *Didache* was considered to have originated with the apostles, its authority was mighty throughout the first millennium of the Church. Many of the early Church fathers quote the document, and some counted it as part of the New Testament.

But while the quotations remained on the record, the documents itself faded from view by the end of the era of the Fathers. Scholars until recently could only speculate about its composition, piecing it together from the various quotations.

Then, in 1873, an orthodox bishop, Metropolitan Philotheos Bryennios, discovered a manuscript of the *Didache* in a library in Constantinople. It was published immediately, to much notice among Christians.

Now, two thousand years after it was written, this ancient catechism has become an important part of the Church's most modern one. And today's Catholics can look into the life and teaching of their first-century forebears, as if in a mirror.

ANTI-CATHOLICISM IN THE ANCIENT WORLD

THE MOST STUBBORN PREJUDICE HAS AN ANCIENT PEDIGREE

"COME, THEN, AFTER YOU HAVE FREED YOURSELF from all the prejudices possessing your mind."

We can take that line, from the second-century Letter to Diognetus, as evidence that anti-Christian prejudice has been with the Church from Day One. In the Roman Empire of those days, pagans caricatured Christian morality as prudery and mocked its mysteries as nonsense. Christian religion was often confused and conflated, in Roman and Greek accounts, with Judaism and the myriad "mystery cults" thriving in Asia Minor at the time.

But amid the babble and bigotry came a group of early Church fathers known as "the apologists." Following St. Peter's counsel, they sought always to "be prepared to make a defense to anyone who calls you to account for the hope that is in you" (1 Pet. 3:15). Some, like Justin Martyr (c. 100–c.165), spoke the highly technical language of the Platonist philosophers, who were somewhat confused about the Christianity they sought to refute. Others spoke to Jews, and still others to the devotees of the mystery cults.

But one apologist offered a different method. He produced a documentary of sorts—a vivid, impressionistic account of how the earliest Christians *really* behaved. In the face of hatred, he showed a community that lived in true love.

We don't know his name, the author who wrote the stunning *Letter to Diognetus*. But he was addressing a high Roman official, and deferentially, assuming that the great Diognetus was intelligent and open-minded (and, certainly, that God's grace was all-powerful).

"I see thee, most excellent Diognetus, exceedingly desirous to learn the mode of worshiping God prevalent among the Christians, and inquiring very carefully and earnestly concerning them, what God they trust in, and what form of religion they observe."

Christianity was a curiosity then, when this author set his stylus to parchment. He refers to the Faith as "this new kind of practice [that] has only now entered into the world." Scholars say the *Letter to Diognetus* was composed in the first half of the second century in Athens, Greece.

The most venturesome dare to attribute the letter to the first known Christian apologist, St. Quadratus (died c. 129), a bishop of Athens and a disciple of the Apostles. There is almost no documentary evidence for this claim, except that early Christian writers refer to a brilliant letter that St. Quadratus wrote to the Roman Emperor Hadrian around 124 in defense of the Faith. And the *Letter to Diognetus* is nothing if not brilliant, in both style and substance.

The letter assumes that its reader has heard, and perhaps believes, many of the common rumors and misunderstandings about Christianity. So the author is careful to distinguish Christianity, first from the other pagan religions, then from Judaism.

One obvious belief that set Christians apart from ordinary Roman citizens was monotheism. Our first forebears in the Faith steadfastly refused to worship idols. Yet other citizens of the empire, the "Letter" points out, were only too willing to bow down before gods of silver, gold, brass, wood and earthenware. In describing these idols, the writer goes into some detail about six shrines, perhaps describing specific temples in the city of Athens.

"Are they not all liable to rot?" he concludes. "Are they not all corruptible, these things you call gods?" The author points out that such polymorphous polytheism had become a cynical and even contemptuous practice for the Romans. Yet, he goes on, "you (Romans) hate the Christians because they do not deem as gods" the idols in the pagan shrines.

For their intransigent monotheism, and their reverence for the Hebrew Scriptures, Christians were often called a Jewish sect. The writer of the *Letter* acknowledges this and praises the Jews for resisting pagan temptations. Yet, he insists, Christians are *not* Jews. First, he says, the "blood and the smoke" of the Temple sacrifices has been surpassed by the sacrifice of Jesus Christ. Next, he points out that the prescriptions of the Law and the rabbinical tradition— regarding circumcision, diet and Sabbath observance—were considered obsolete by Christians.

Yet, if Christians were not pagans and not Jews, who were they? That is the subject of the final section of the epistle.

In this section the author overwhelms his reader, not so much with dogma, but with small glimpses of the everyday life of the Church's founding families.

First of all, he says, you can't tell a Christian just by looking. "For the Christians are distinguished from other men neither by country, nor language, nor the customs which they observe. They neither inhabit cities of their own, nor employ a peculiar form of speech, nor lead a life which is marked out by any singularity . . . [They follow] the customs of the natives in respect to clothing, food and the rest of their ordinary conduct."

Christians blend in, he says—to a point.

Where they are set apart is in their charity for each other and their upright moral behavior. Here, the *Letter* writer makes more important distinctions.

Christianity did not, as some rumors claimed, entail severe asceticism and universal celibacy. The *Letter* explains that Christians, like everyone else, "marry and beget children." Yet they differ essentially from the merely worldly because Christians reject immoral pagan practices, such as abortion and infanticide. Christians "do not destroy their offspring," the *Letter* states. Nor did Christians sleep around, as the pagans did: "They have a common table, but not a common bed."

Christians are good for the economy and the social order, the *Letter* claims. Believers, after all, "obey the prescribed laws, and at the same time surpass the laws by their lives . . . They are poor, yet make many rich." And good Christians don't make trouble for the pagans, the *Letter* writer seems to say, even though pagans often make trouble for Christians. "They love all men, and are persecuted by all . . . they are insulted, and repay the insult with honour . . . When punished, they rejoice as if quickened into life."

Our author follows this with his most remarkable statement: "To sum it up—what the soul is in the body, Christians are in the world." According to this ancient Athenian, Christians, then, are the life-giving principle in the world. You can't see them—but without them, the whole human enterprise is doomed.

"The soul is dispersed through all the members of the body, and Christians are scattered through all the cities of the world. The soul dwells in the body, yet is not of the body; and Christians dwell in the world, yet are not of the world. . . . The soul, when but ill-provided with food and drink, becomes better; in like manner, Christians, though subjected day by day to punishment, increase the more in number."

What gives Christians strength to live this way? Our correspondent gives a brief, but breathless testimony to the divine origin of the Christian faith. Without this faith, he demonstrates, all humankind, through all history, has dwelt in misery.

Then the *Letter* ends in the only way such a Christian testimony can, with a plea to Diognetus (the debauched, homosexual Emperor Hadrian?) for personal conversion.

"With what joy do you think you will be filled? Or how will you love him who has first so loved you? If you love him, you will be an imitator of his kindness. And do not wonder that a man may become an imitator of God. He can, if he is willing. For it is not by ruling over his neighbors, . . . that happiness is found. . . . On the contrary he who takes upon himself the burden of his neighbor . . . by distributing to the needy, becomes a god to those who receive."

If Diognetus or Hadrian were not convinced, many more would be. If not by a letter, then by the lives of so many anonymous Christians. Just a few centuries after the *Letter* was composed, the pagan West passed away. Yet the *Letter,* providentially, lived on till very recently.

Then, in 1870, the only surviving manuscript of the *Letter* was destroyed. Today, perhaps the pagan West is returning, and a billion invisible Catholics—the soul of the modern world—must write the letter anew, now as then, in the everyday details of their ordinary lives.

APOCRYPHA NOW!

IS OUR CANON TOO CRAMPED?

AFTER A SIXTEEN HUNDRED YEAR MARKET LULL, gospels are once again a growth industry.

Publishers now are rushing to supplement the only standbys—Matthew, Mark, Luke and John—with some ancient castoffs: the so-called gospels of Judas, Mary Magdalene, Thomas, and Philip, among others.

These are the "apocryphal" ("hidden") gospels, purported portraits of Jesus that were spurned as phony or heretical by the early Church. For years, they were a curiosity indulged only by scholars. Now, they're making a popular comeback.

Browse your local bookstores, and you'll likely find a dozen collections of apocrypha, most of them released by major publishers in the last five years. Titles are provocative: *The Other Bible*, *The Complete Gospels*, *The Hidden Teachings of Jesus*, and *The Lost Books of the Bible*. All suggest that the standard Christian Bible is missing something essential. One volume boasts that it contains "Everything you need to empower your own search for the historical Jesus."

Many Catholic scholars, however, dismiss the fad. "I can't believe this is happening," said Father Peter Stravinskas, author of *The Catholic Church and the Bible.* "When I was in grade school, some sisters would tell us syrupy stories from the infancy gospels, and they would be reprimanded by their superiors for teaching such nonsense."

The infancy gospels—fanciful accounts of Jesus' childhood—make up just one category of apocryphal literature. There are also collections of Jesus' alleged sayings, full-scale biographies, apocalyptic tracts (similar in style to the biblical Book of Revelation) and letters attributed to the apostles.

Most arose in the first three centuries of Christianity, before the Church officially proclaimed the "canon," or definitive list of New Testament books.

Some of the apocrypha were dismissed out of hand by the Fathers of the Church because of the narratives' patent absurdity or crude style. Others were seriously considered for inclusion in the canon, but were eventually dropped because their contents did not stand up to scrutiny.

Lists had long been in use in local churches. A Milanese fragment, the Muratorian Canon, survives from the second century. And St. Athanasius, in the mid-fourth century, published a list that is identical with New Testament as we know it today. The matter of the Christian canon was definitively settled with the Synods of Hippo (A.D. 393) and Carthage (397 and 419), which were guided by the brilliant St. Augustine. These synods confirmed the list of the Roman synod of 382, attended by Jerome and presided over by Pope Damasus. The same list appeared in a letter of Pope Innocent I in 405. Rome had spoken; the matter was settled, right?

Well, sort of. Even afterward, however, some Christian apocrypha continued to influence popular piety and art. Yet few people seriously considered these "gospels" sacred, or even historically reliable—until recently.

Some years back I interviewed William Farmer, who was then the general editor of the International Bible Commentary. Farmer (a remarkable scholar, who has since passed away) traced the resurgence of interest in Christian apocrypha to an archeological find in 1945: "The single most important factor has been the discovery of the fourth-century Nag Hammadi library in Egypt. The texts included a copy of the Gospel of Thomas, a collection of purported sayings of Jesus."

Scholars differ on the exact date of the Gospel of Thomas, but most agree that it is of great antiquity. Some—though not in the mainstream—believe it to be older than books that were included in the New Testament.

The Gospel of Thomas, like all the texts in the Nag Hammadi cache, is Gnostic in character. Gnosticism, a religious movement contemporary with early Christianity, held that salvation came through secret knowledge (in Greek, *gnosis*) given only to a spiritual elite. Gnostic Christians, whom the Church rejected early as heretics, taught that Jesus' mission was to reveal this secret knowledge and separate the saved "knowers" from the ignorant rabble.

Most Gnostics took a dim view of the material world and especially of the human body, which they saw as a prison for the spirit. As a result, they minimized (or denied) the importance of Jesus' bodily incarnation, His suffering and His Resurrection, emphasizing instead His spiritual reality and teaching. Thus they also minimized the uniqueness of the witness of the twelve apostles.

Gnostic Christians taught, instead, that any one of the elite could have a spiritual encounter with Jesus and write a "gospel" that was just as authoritative as those by the apostles.

And write them they did—leading St. Irenaeus to complain in 180 that "every one of them generates something new, day by day, according to his ability; for no one is deemed perfect who does not develop some mighty fictions."[1]

The Nag Hammadi find included mighty fictions attributed to James, John, Peter, Paul, Thomas and Mary Magdalene. Some thirty years after their discovery, the texts reached a wide audience through Elaine Pagels' popular paperback *The Gnostic Gospels*, which some critics described as an "altar call" for a Gnostic revival.

Pagels, however, did explain why the institutional Church could not peacefully coexist with Gnostic members.

The Church proclaimed universal salvation, while Gnostics reserved the gift only for an elite. The Church taught that the death and Resurrection of Jesus were decisive historic events; Gnostics saw them as metaphors or illusions. The Church looked to the apostles for authority, while Gnostics looked in the mirror.

St. Irenaeus railed against Gnostic arrogance: "They consider themselves mature so that no one can be compared with them in the greatness of their knowledge, not Peter or Paul or any other apostles!"

The most famous Gnostic gospel, that of Thomas, is a collection of sayings, some of which also appear in the canonical Gospels, while others portray a Jesus unrecognizable—a savior who denies He is "master" to His followers.

---

1   St. Irenaeus of Lyons, *Against the Heresies* 1.18.1.

Yet "Thomas" has gained a following, recently, among fringe groups in academia. The Jesus Seminar, a free-standing research institute, published Thomas with the four canonical Gospels in a single volume titled *The Five Gospels.*

Father Alfred McBride, O. Praem., author of many Catholic Scripture studies, sees the book's title as significant. "Those who speak for the Jesus Seminar show a great deal of interest in elevating Thomas to canonical status," he told me in a 1998 interview. "And in so doing they reduce the importance and authority of the present New Testament canon. They have their reasons: Thomas has no Passion narratives, no miracles, not much that's supernatural. It's Jesus the wisdom teacher, which suits their idea that religion is merely humanitarian common sense."

Participants in the Jesus Seminar also produced *The Complete Gospels,* an anthology of more than a dozen apocrypha packaged with the canonical four—implying a level playing field for what they call alternative "early Jesus traditions." Yet they fail to emphasize that the apocryphal gospels rarely gained more than small, local followings, and that many were condemned as heretical from the get-go, while others were dismissed as inaccurate or tawdry.

The Gospel of Nicodemus, for example, is a moving courtroom drama, attempting to portray the small details of Jesus' trial before Pilate. Doctrinally, it checks out; stylistically, it passes muster. But ultimately it failed the test for the Church fathers because it is wildly inaccurate in its depiction of Roman jurisprudence and Jewish custom. It also stretches credulity by purporting to describe Jesus' descent into hell.

"You find a tendency toward sensationalism in the apocrypha," said Father Stravinskas. "In the canonical Gospels, there's a reverential silence on some matters. The apocrypha, however, are ebullient in divulging intimate details about Our Lady and Our Lord."

Indeed, while canonical Luke and Matthew merely state that Mary is a virgin, the author of Infancy-James goes so far as to drag in a skeptical midwife to perform a physical examination.

The boy Jesus, for His part, appears in the infancy gospels as a sort of wonder-working Dennis the Menace. In Infancy-Thomas, Jesus breathes life into clay birds, stretches beams in His father's carpentry shop and strikes dead a teacher who dared to punish Him. In the Arabic Infancy Gospel, He turns cruel playmates into goats. According to Infancy-Thomas, the boy's neighbors lived in constant fear, moving St. Joseph to cry out: "Do not let [Jesus] go outside the door, because anyone who angers Him dies!"

More troubling, the Nag Hammadi Gospel of Philip strongly suggests that Jesus was physically intimate with Mary Magdalene: "Christ loved her more than all the disciples," it alleges, "and used to kiss her often on the mouth."

Most of the apocrypha offer not a different perspective on the historical Jesus, but rather a different Jesus, and some, indeed, purvey a different religion.

According to Father Stravinskas, this accounts for some of their appeal today. "This is a resurgence of Gnosticism," he said. "These people claim to have a better grasp of the truth than anyone else in the Church, including the magisterium."

He said the apocrypha also appeal to prurient interests of more mainstream Catholics: "It's in synch with a tendency to rely on extraordinary revelations: apparitions, visionaries and messages of a doomsday nature."

Father McBride pointed out that the marketing of these books relies on anti-Catholicism to tease readers with a taste of forbidden fruit. "The message is that the Catholic Church has been keeping secrets, once again chaining up the Bible, not letting people know the real story."

But, for scholars, the recent surge of interest presents an opportunity, according to Farmer, who enjoyed a distinguished career in biblical studies at Southern Methodist University and converted late in life to Catholicism. "The emergence of these new materials gives us an opportunity to develop a deeper understanding of the canon," he said. "I hope that Christians who regard the canon as decisive for faith might come to a better understanding of why the Church has preserved some books and not others."

Still, all the dialogue in the academy won't change the list of approved books, Farmer said. And Father McBride agreed: "The canon belongs to the Church, not the university."

Father Stravinskas explained why: "Karl Rahner said that the Church, in deciding the canon, was like a mother at work in her apartment, and down below in the courtyard there could be forty children screaming or crying— but she could hear the voice of her own and know it."

ICONS

WINDOWS ON ANOTHER WORLD

IT'S NOT OFTEN AT ART EXHIBITS that you see passersby moved to tears, bowing in prayer, crossing themselves or whispering devotions.

Yet so it was at New York's Metropolitan Museum of Art, as thousands filed past the images of Christ and the Virgin, the saints and the angels, showing in "The Glory of Byzantium," which I visited back in 1997.

Though the exhibit included works of pottery, sculpture, tapestry and bookbinding, the dominant form, by far, was the icon, the traditional type of sacred image in Eastern Christianity.

Indeed, many of those who filed through, rapt in prayer, seem to be Eastern Christians—Orthodox or Catholics of the Eastern Rites. While a museum docent led groups through and spoke with erudition of a mosaic's "evocation of the numinous," her onlookers themselves appeared to be caught up in the numinous.

For icons are more than art. In the Eastern Church, they are central to the practice of the Faith. One saint called them "open books that remind us of God." Tradition refers to them as "windows on another world."

The term "icon" properly refers to works produced by certain formal techniques, hallowed by almost two thousand years of tradition in the East.

The Middle Byzantine period, the time covered by the Met's exhibit, is known as the golden age of icon production.

Icons range in style, though they share some common characteristics: a two-dimensional quality, symbolic use of color and shape, and surreal, slightly distorted bodily and facial features: elongated fingers, impossibly large eyes, long necks.

They are essentially different from Western religious art, which is almost always associated with an individual creative genius: Giotto, say, or Michelangelo or Rembrandt. Not so with iconography: Most Middle Byzantine iconographers remained anonymous. Their work is impersonal, adhering to strict forms that manifest the heavenly archetypes. In some monasteries, painters specialized—one monk for eyes, another for hands, another for hair—so that no single artist could claim a work for his own.

Still, such work required a high level of technical skill. Icons speak a rich, symbolic language. Every color, gesture, garment, shadow and prop is significant . . . The oversized eyes? They represent the beatific vision of God that a saint enjoys in heaven. A sideward gaze? The aloofness and peace of someone who has left behind the cares of the world. The bright gold background? The divine aura, the glorious atmosphere of heaven.

In any good library you'll find thick volumes that explain how to "read" icons. But no one really needs a lexicon. For two millennia, icons have served as the theology textbook of the saints, the catechism of the unlettered, and the pauper's psalter.

From the icon of the *Pantocrator* (Lord of the Universe), the faithful gain confidence to abandon themselves to a Will that is all-powerful and all-good. From the *Eleousa* (Virgin of Tenderness), they learn of humility, selflessness and the maternal care of the Mother of God. From the *Man of Sorrows*, they see the redemptive value of suffering.

The saints of the East bring up another important lesson taught by icons: that every man and woman is an icon of God—made in the divine image and likeness.

That's the sort of radical doctrine that has made icons the target of puritan purges down through the ages. In the eighth and ninth centuries, the puritans were running the Byzantine Empire. They called themselves iconoclasts ("icon-smashers"), because they believed that the veneration of icons violated the first commandment's prohibition of "graven images." They accused their opponents of worshiping wood and pigment. And they had other items on their agenda: Some iconoclasts believed that all matter was contemptible and so doubted that Christ was truly human, as the Bible and the Church fathers had taught.

A holy monk, St. John of Damascus (675–749)—the last of the Eastern Fathers—wrote a devastating refutation of the iconoclasts' position, showing that it opposed Scripture, tradition and good sense. A capsule of his hundred or so pages: "In former times, God, being without form or body, could in no way be represented. But today, since God has appeared in the flesh and lived among men, I can represent what is visible in God. I do not worship matter, but I worship the creator of matter who became matter for my sake . . . and who, through matter, accomplished my salvation. Never will I cease to honor the matter which brought about my salvation!"

With the Council of Nicea, in 787, the Church declared definitively in favor of icons: "Holy icons ought to be exposed to view, since the more Jesus Christ, His mother and the saints are seen in their likeness, the more will people be led to think of the originals and to love them. Honor is paid to icons, but not worship, which belongs to God alone. Honor paid to images is directed to the original which they represent."

Yet the prohibition of images continued until the rise of the "iconodule" (image-loving) regent Theodora. Her proclamation restoring icons in 843 is today commemorated in the Eastern Church by a special feast day.

The Second-Nicene Fathers, like John of Damascus before them, were always careful to remind us that in icons we see "as through a glass, darkly."

MEMORIAL DAYS, FROM TIME IMMEMORIAL

AS THE YEAR WINDS DOWN, WE REMEMBER OUR DEAD— all saints, all souls. By this very practice we honor the Fathers, because they themselves taught us to do it, beginning with the first generations of the Church.

There's a sense in which the early Christians kept every day as a "Memorial Day." They called the Eucharist a "memorial" of Christ's death—a God-willed remembrance through which Jesus became really present. And at Mass they marked not only Christ's death, but also the days of the saints who died in Christ, especially the martyrs. Very early, the Church's calendar began to teem with feast days honoring the dead, and the living Christians gained some notoriety for their treatment of the deceased.

Cremation had long been the norm in pagan societies. Jews, however, followed the custom of burying their dead. Christians did, too, and looked upon "Christian burial" as an expression of their faith in the resurrection of the body. Such an oddity was this practice that, in many locales, it earned Christians a derogatory nickname: "The Diggers."

Yet the pagans also honored their dead, often with lavish funeral rites. Roman families hosted several banquets to honor their recently deceased: one at the gravesite the day of the funeral; the second at the end of nine days of mourning; others on specified religious holidays; and one major banquet on the birthday of the deceased.

Christians adapted the custom of funerary banquets. In some places they may have taken the form of an "Agape," or love-feast, as we find recorded in the New Testament Epistle of St. Jude. Another possibility is that the funeral Eucharist was observed as part of a fuller banquet, such as we find in St. Paul's First Letter to the Corinthians (chapter 11). In some churches the funeral was certainly marked by a Eucharist at the gravesite. We have a very early record of the graveside practice, from the mid-second century, in the apocryphal Acts of John. These funerary banquets or Masses may also be the meals we find depicted on the walls of the catacombs.

By the fourth century, the gravesite celebrations—sometimes called *refrigeria*, or "refreshments"—had gained a reputation in some quarters as raucous, drunken affairs. This was especially true of the festivals of popular saints, where the temptation was strong to knock one back for every glass poured out as a libation. When St. Monica moved from North Africa to Italy to be near her son Augustine, the Milanese bishop, St. Ambrose, discouraged her from observing the *refrigeria* at all—even in a pious way.

The liturgical scholar Joseph Jungmann noted that the earliest recorded graveside Masses were offered on the third day after the Christian's burial. The third day—what a stunning symbolic fulfillment of our life in Christ! Jungmann sees this custom as the ancestor of our current practice of votive Masses for the dead. And he notes times and places where various churches traditionally observed the seventh day, the ninth, the thirtieth, and the fortieth as well.

Some people see the gorgeous farewell passage in Augustine's *Confessions* as a turning point in ancient attitudes. There, Monica, who had once avidly marked the *refrigerium*, now asks her son to remember her in the Mass. It is, they say, at this moment in history that popular sentiment had begun to turn from the rowdy festival to the solemn Mass. That's a nice thought, but it seems contradicted by later practice, as Christians continued to mark festive banquets at gravesites throughout the era of the Fathers.

Some years ago, as I walked through the ancient burial grounds of the Roman Church, I had a "Christmas Carol" moment straight out of Dickens.

At the Catacombs of St. Callixtus, I wandered into a "Crypt of Refrigerium" that bore the inscription *Aquilina dormit in pace* (translation: "Aquilina sleeps in peace").

May that inscription one day be true for me, and may it this day be true of my ancestors, whom I remember, as the seasons require.

FOUR GREAT BOOKS

1. *THE CHRISTIAN CATACOMBS OF ROME: HISTORY, DECORATION, INSCRIPTIONS*

The Roman catacombs are a veritable city of the dead. More than sixty miles of labyrinthine corridors have been discovered so far, and archeologists are still finding more. Estimates of their population range into the millions. And they are our richest source of evidence of early Christian life.

A lavishly illustrated coffee-table volume, *The Christian Catacombs of Rome: History, Decoration, Inscriptions* (*Schnell & Steiner, 2006*), allows us to walk those corridors with three of the world's leading experts on the subject: Vincenzo Fiocchi Nicolai, Fabrizio Bisconti, and Danilo Mazzoleni. All are members of the Vatican's Pontifical Commission on Sacred Archeology; all teach archeology at Roman universities.

From their intimate knowledge of thousands of inscriptions, artifacts, bone fragments, and artworks, the authors give us brief and brilliant glimpses of the ordinary lives of the early Christians, answering questions like: What kind of work did they do? Were they poor, rich, or middle-class? (See below.) How old were they when they married? (Women were 14–20, men 20–30.) What qualities did they value in their spouses and in their children? (No surprise here: fidelity, affability, concord, integrity.) How did they die? (Relatively few were martyrs.)

The catacombs were dug by a professional corps of tunnelers out of the soft volcanic rock at the outskirts of Rome. Following soon after were an army of artists and artisans: brick masons, stone masons, plasterers, sculptors, mosaic and fresco artists, not to mention priests and mourners.

And much of this industry bustled during a time of intermittent persecution. Though the Christian catacombs represent the first massive public work of the Church, they were, so to speak, an underground economy.

The book divides neatly into three sections. Vincenzo Fiocchi Nicolai sketches the catacombs' origin and development, giving readers a concise but complete introduction to the subject. He covers not only the history of their construction, but also the history of their excavation—which, given the crude methods of past centuries, was sometimes their destruction.

In the second section, Fabrizio Bisconti examines the artistic decoration of the catacombs and its interpretation (a field given to much controversy). In the final section, Danilo Mazzoleni highlights the forty thousand inscriptions that embellish the tombs, inscriptions that range from graffiti scratched in plaster to poems chiseled in marble.

All three sections are packed with useful and fascinating details. Mazzoleni, for example, uses the epitaphs to show us what the early Christians did for a living. They were "bricklayers, cleaners, dyers, seamstresses, shoemakers and cobblers . . . doctors and veterinarians, lawyers, notaries, stenographers, couriers, teachers, and clerks of grain administration." Thus, we see the whole range of professions and social classes, and probably in close proportion to their distribution in Roman society.

Along the way, he challenges the fairly common assertion that the pre-Constantinian Christians were overwhelmingly pacifist. On the contrary, he writes, "diverse specialties and every rank" of the military are represented in Christian catacomb inscriptions, "including praetorians (the corps was disbanded by Constantine), cavalry and equites singulares."

Mazzoleni also analyzes the names bestowed and taken by the Christians of Rome. Readers can follow the trends through those early centuries, learning, for example, that relatively few chose biblical names, and many chose the names of martyrs (there are three thousand Lawrences in one catacomb alone!). It was more common, however, to choose names with theological associations, such as Agape (love), Irene (peace), Anastasius (resurrection), Spes (hope), Quodvultdeus (what God wills), and so on. And many Christians seem to have stuck with the old, traditional Roman names, the names of pagan deities (Hermes, Hercules, Aphrodite, Eros).

One illuminating subsection covers "Humiliating names or nicknames." These names "were sometimes used by some faithful as a life-long act of modesty, precisely because of their unpleasant significance . . . This is the case of *Proiectus* and *Proiecticus*, which meant 'exposed,' and the unpleasant *Stercorius*, [which] can be understood as 'abandoned in the garbage.' . . . At the Catacomb of Pretestato, one of them was in fact named *Stercorinus*."

The authors (or translators) are being polite. Stercorius is most accurately translated by what kids call "the S-word." Thus, *Stercorinus* (the diminutive) means "Little S***," or "Dear S***."

Why would Christians bear such a name? It is likely that these particular Romans were, as infants, rescued from the dungheap—the place where Romans abandoned "defective" or female newborns. After all, the pagan philosopher Seneca said: "What is good must be set apart from what is good-for-nothing."

I'll bet that no small number of those "good-for-nothings" were rescued by Christian families. They were lucky to be alive, but surely they still had to suffer the taunts of playmates, who were pleased to remind them of their lowly origins.

As Mazzoleni points out, they may have kept those demeaning names as "a life-long act of modesty"—or perhaps as an act of triumphant irony. The joke, after all, was on the pagan world, which would soon enough die out for the crime of murdering its young. These children who were dung in the eyes of Imperial Rome knew that they were precious in the sight of God.

And in the catacombs they were buried among popes and praetorian guards. Nicolai remarks on the "uniformity of the tombs" that demonstrates the "heavily egalitarian ideology of the new religion." In the catacombs, Stercorius is immortal, even in a merely historical sense, thanks to the work of these three authors. Reading their book is a profoundly religious experience.

2. THE SPIRIT OF EARLY CHRISTIAN THOUGHT: SEEKING THE FACE OF GOD

Sooner or later, every thinking Christian discovers the duty to study the Church fathers. It presents itself as a matter of religious literacy, if not a debt of ancestral piety. They fought the first culture wars; we should at least learn from them. They died for our faith; we should at least honor their memory.

Now comes the dean of America's Church historians to turn our duty to pleasure and our debt to our profit.

Robert Louis Wilken has produced a masterly appreciation of the Fathers in *The Spirit of Early Christian Thought: Seeking the Face of God* (Yale, 2003). And it is an unabashed *appreciation*. Longtime readers of Wilken will see here the love that has animated four decades of serious and dispassionate scholarship. First-time readers will wish to spend at least the next several decades reading the works that have inspired Wilken's love.

Synthesizing the Fathers can be a bit chaotic. The last Fathers (in the eighth century) are as far from the first as we are from Dante. They ranged over thousands of square miles and several major language groups, and they held forth on matters as varied as capital punishment and the morality of bathing. They were no more uniform in temperament, and one of the great virtues of this book is its artful evocation of their variety. Though he depends most often on four ancient writers—Origen, Gregory of Nyssa, Augustine, and Maximus—Wilken vividly sketches dozens of other personalities: Clement, Justin, Ambrose, Hilary, Basil, John of Damascus, Cyril of Alexandria, and several men named Gregory.

But how to bring it all together? Wilken's approach is thematic rather than chronological, and the overarching theme is the Fathers' response to the Incarnation of God in Jesus Christ. That event, that fact, affected everything in the Fathers' world. "Because of the Incarnation," Wilken explains, "Christianity posits an intimate relation between material things and the living God."

Thus, the Faith found expression not merely in argument, but in every aspect of culture. Wilken protests that "the study of early Christian thought has been too preoccupied with ideas"—the cascading influence from one theologian to another and another. There are other ways of thinking, and especially of thinking about faith, and Wilken takes these up one by one.

There arose, for example, a distinctively Christian sort of poetry and painting, and each merits its own chapter. These arts, too, appear as consequences of the Incarnation. Wilken says, more than once in this book, that "Christianity is an affair of things," and so he shows how the early Christians sanctified the aural pleasures of scansion, the visual delights of iconography.

Wilken shows the cultural triumph of Christianity as something gradual, but inexorable, proceeding according to the incarnational principle. He is fond of the word "inevitability" and applies it to areas that some modern Christians will find unnerving, as when he speaks of "the inevitability of allegory" and "the inevitability of authority." But he follows the Fathers closely as they demonstrate how these, and many other Christian developments, follow in a reasonable way from the teaching of Christ in the Scriptures.

There are those, of course, who see the Fathers as a world apart from Scripture. There are those who say the Fathers represent the Greeking of a primitive and purely semitic Christian religion.

But Wilken isn't one of those. In fact, he begins with the assumption that they are wrong: "Christian thinking is too independent to be treated chiefly in relation to Greco-Roman thought," he writes in his introduction. And the rest of the book shows how wrong they are. "The notion that the development of early Christian thought represented a hellenization of Christianity has outlived its usefulness. . . . a more apt expression would be the Christianization of Hellenism."

The Fathers we meet in Wilken's book (and meet them we do, as vividly as we'd meet a colorful new neighbor or colleague) are men steeped in the Scriptures, formed by the Scriptures, inebriated by the Scriptures. "Early Christian thought," says Wilken, "is biblical, and one of the lasting accomplishments of the patristic period was to forge a way of thinking, scriptural in language and inspiration, that gave to the Church and to Western civilization a unified and coherent interpretation of the Bible as a whole."

The Fathers assimilated the Scriptures and preached them in a way that was culture-forming, not Bible-thumping. "Even the Bible was a book to be argued from," Wilken explains, "not simply an authority to brandish when arguments failed. Origen's assertion that the gospel had a 'proof proper to itself' was not a confession of faith, but the beginning of an argument."

There was an implied apologetic in the works of the Fathers: "Their goal was to forge a view of creation and of human beings that was biblical, yet intelligible and coherent to all reasonable persons."

Ultimately, the Fathers achieved that goal. Wilken counts this as a good thing. (Indeed, the *New York Times*, in a bizarre review, faulted him for his unambiguous joy over Christianity's success—"unmistakably confessional triumphalism," they called it—and for not boring his intended audience, "the general reader," with scholarly quibbles and minutiae. Alas.)

In succeeding, however, the Fathers showed that those pagans were right who saw the Church as subversive. Wilken even grants us the pleasure of meeting those pagans personally. One of the marvels of charity in this book is the genuine sympathy the author shows for the reasoning of the archvillains of early Christian history, Celsus and Julian. Those men were right about one thing at least: Christianity, when it is true, cannot help but transform a culture.

3. THROUGH THEIR OWN EYES: LITURGY AS THE BYZANTINES SAW IT

Despite the civil unrest in the late 1950s, a young Jesuit priest serving a parish in Bahgdad traveled the Iraqi countryside observing the liturgies of the Syriac-speaking villages and monasteries. And there Robert Taft, S.J., got hooked on liturgics. Since then, he's written about three dozen books and several hundred articles on the ancient rites and the Fathers.

A longtime professor of liturgy and patristics at the Pontifical Oriental Institute in Rome, he is a Catholic priest of both the Latin and Byzantine rites. (And yes, he is indeed part of the family that produced several illustrious American statesmen, including one president.)

It would be an understatement to say that Taft is outspoken. He has a first-rate mind, and he speaks it with force and wit. Read his 2004 interview with John Allen in the *National Catholic Reporter*. It is the very image of a loose cannon rolling down the tilting deck of the barque of Peter and firing away. I'm sure it sent several dozen ecumenists into damage-control mode for weeks afterward.

His academic work has been a little more restrained in expression, but no less certain in its conclusions.

But his most recent book, *Through Their Own Eyes: Liturgy as the Byzantines Saw It* (InterOrthodox Press, 2006), now that's another story. Made up of edited transcripts of his 2005 Paul G. Manolis Distinguished

Lectures at the Patriarch Athenagoras Orthodox Institute in Berkeley, California, this book combines the academic rigor of the published Taft with the frankness of his live lectures.

It is a book by turns moving and entertaining. Father Taft sets out to give us a "bottom-up" view of the Byzantine liturgy, as it was experienced by the congregations of late antiquity, rather than as explicated by the Church fathers. The situation was, as he points out, "not all incense and icons."

Citing the Great Fathers, he evokes free-ranging congregations where young men and women trolled the crowd for romance. Chrysostom complained that the women at church were no different from courtesans, and the men like "frantic stallions." He also noted that people were talking throughout the liturgy, and "their talk is filthier than excrement." Old Golden Mouth went on to report that the rush for Communion proceeded by way of "kicking, striking, filled with anger, shoving our neighbors, full of disorder."

It almost makes today's American Catholic parishes look reverent.

Taft walks us through the liturgy, from introit to dismissal, in a kind of reverse mystagogy. Traditional mystagogy—that is, instruction in the mysteries—begins with the outward signs and proceeds to their hidden meaning. Taft, however, begins with the assumption that the liturgy is heavenly; and then he shows us the very incarnational, very earthly (and earthy) details of the scene where the liturgy touches down. At each stage, he quotes from contemporary accounts of what was going on in the assembly. We learn about the vigorous singing, the popularity of the Psalms, the entertainment value of a sonorous homily, even if it's in an archaic language that no one understands.

Liturgy was central to life in the big city. Entire populations turned out for icon processions and for the movement of relics. Sometimes, these mass liturgical rallies turned into mob scenes as the herd stampeded toward the center of grace. He brings up the fourth-century pilgrim Egeria's story about the man who bit off a piece of the true cross to take home as a souvenir.

And yet, for all that, "the Church's earthly song of praise is but an icon, the reflection—in the Pauline sense of mysterion, a visible appearance that is bearer of the reality it represents—of the heavenly liturgy of the Risen Lord before the throne of God. As such, it is an ever-present, vibrant participation in the heavenly worship of God's Son."

"Byzantine art and ritual," Taft says as he brings his final lecture to its conclusion, "far from being all ethereal and spiritual and transcendent and symbolic, was in fact a very concrete attempt at portrayal, at opening a window onto the sacred, of bridging the gap."

Even the best dressed and best behaved among us are oafs and waifs pressing our dirty noses against the window. If we spend our hour of worship worrying about the comportment of the Joneses in the next pew, we're missing the point of worship.

Taft's book offers a good counter-balance for those who feed off the liturgical works of Ambrose, Cyril, and Theodore (though we do get a hint of the underside in Augustine). Taft confesses that he himself has written books romanticizing the ancient liturgies. Perhaps *Through Their Own Eyes* is his act of reparation. In any event, it's our gain.

This book will inflame passions all around. For one thing, it includes the transcripts of the question-and-answer periods after the lectures, and there the erudite father does not mince words as he asserts the appropriateness of the vernacular, the "stupidity" of the trend toward more variety in liturgy, and so on.

But whether you agree with Taft or not, his new book will give you an experience of time travel. And a joy ride.

4. *THE LAST PAGAN* AND *THE LAST ROMAN*

The Fall of Rome is, for the educated Westerner, like the Fall of Man. We know we must come to terms with it. But when we face those thick volumes of Gibbon we wish it didn't have to be such a wearisome task.

Now Scottish historian Adrian Murdoch comes along to turn our burdens into purely pleasurable reading. He comes well trained for the task. A fellow of the British Royal Historical Society, Murdoch is also a prominent journalist, covering international affairs and economics in the mainstream press. Thus, he brings to his books a rare combination: the depth of a professional historian and the readability of a newspaper's front page, above the fold.

His most recent books, *The Last Pagan* (Sutton, 2005) and *The Last Roman* (Sutton, 2006), focus on aspects of the empire's end. They are studies of two very different emperors, both of whom ruled after Christianity's "triumph": Julian (known as "the Apostate," reigned 361–363) and Romulus

Augustulus (475–476). Julian was arguably the last ruler to cling to Rome's classical heritage. Romulus was simply the last Roman emperor.

The Last Roman appeared on the market just as Hollywood released its own version of the story of Romulus, *The Last Legion*, with Thomas Sangster as the thirteen-year-old emperor, and Sir Ben Kingsley as his tutor. So perhaps it is best to begin with a discussion of that Romulus, as he's fresh in memory, at least for some readers.

When asked to provide a date for the fall of the Roman Empire, some historians point to the brief (ten-month) reign of Romulus. Barely pubescent, the boy ruled as a mouthpiece for his father, a power-brokering general in the Roman army. The child-emperor, easily removed by the barbarian warlord, is an apt image of the empire at its end. Even the boy's nickname—*Augustulus*, "little Augustus"—suggests the puniness of fifth-century Rome compared to its first-century glory. Murdoch says of Romulus: "It has always been easier and more potent to keep him as the symbol of the end, rather than try to flesh him out as a real person."

Yet Murdoch does the hard historical detective work and traces Romulus' movements through the rest of his probably long life. He seems to have retired to a monastery well stocked with books. "The image of him, an old man in a library in Campania, corresponding with leading intellectuals of the day, his early life and elevation to power becoming an increasingly indistinct memory, is as attractive a thought as the beautiful boy in his teens."

Since so little is known about Romulus, Murdoch must sketch his life in chiaroscuro, finding the boy's life, and then the man's, in the shadows of the barbarian conquerors Odovacer and Theoderic. And the shadows are dark indeed. Against recent historians who argue that the transition from Roman to barbarian rule went fairly smoothly for common folk, Murdoch counters that it was rather catastrophic, beginning with pillage and ending in lawlessness. Murdoch is at his best when describing battles, raids, campaigns, and diplomatic missions. Religion he declares beyond the scope of his study, though he does touch lightly on the differences between the Arian barbarians and the Catholic Romans, and how these played out in the decades after the fall. Along the way he tells the tragic story of Boethius, the most famous victim of Theoderic's growing suspicion of Nicene Christians.

All the ancient voices in this book sound human, a rare quality attributable to Murdoch's ease with ancient languages and his stunning ability to turn a phrase in English. He manages even to replicate wordplay: "Cattily, the poet Martial wrote that women would arrive in the region as a Penelope, the famously chaste wife of Odysseus, and leave a Helen, the much chased wife of Menelaus."

The Last Roman is an important book for its development of the symbol of Rome's fall in the boy-emperor Romulus. But the more potent book by far is the biography of the more potent ruler, Julian, *The Last Pagan*.

Though he ruled less than three years, Julian looms colossal in memory and imagination.

He was born in 331 (or 332) into a brutal family and a bloody business. His father was Emperor Constantine's half-brother. Murdoch notes that, after Diocletian's retirement in 305, "Julian's family spent a great deal of the next fifty years developing ingenious ways to kill each other." The motive was usually intrigue, plots for accession, or just the suspicion bred by such an atmosphere. In 326, Constantine ordered the execution of his wife and eldest son. The three remaining sons succeeded their father in 337 and rather quickly dispatched almost all their male relatives. Two young boys were spared, five-year-old Julian and his teenage brother Gallus. Julian was too young to be a threat and Gallus too sickly. Though Julian continued to live the privileged life of the imperial family, he kept the memory of that purge, whose victims included his own father. Years later, he would write with incredulity of his cousin, Emperor Constantius: "Our fathers were brothers, sons of the same father. And close relations as we were, how this most humane emperor treated us. He put to death six of our cousins, my father who was his uncle, another of our uncles on my father's side and my eldest brother, without trial."

The imperial family was officially Christian by this time, and the irony was not lost on Julian, who was himself raised a Christian, and was a schoolmate of St. Basil the Great and St. Gregory Nazianzus. Constantius the murderer professed the doctrine of Jesus Christ. It doesn't take a psychiatrist to locate the origins of Julian's anti-Christian animus.

But Julian learned to keep his thoughts largely to himself. Constantius was his patron, and alienation from him meant certain death. Julian studied philosophy and rhetoric at Athens and secretly investigated the "old religion," the pagan mysteries. Though he kept up his exterior practice of Christianity, his mind and heart belonged to the old gods.

Appointed to leadership in the military, Julian rose rapidly with some stunning campaigns in the western provinces and barbarian lands. He gained a reputation for toughness; for, unlike other generals, he shared the hardships of his troops. He ate what they ate; slept where they slept. And he rewarded them handsomely. All this made for tenacious loyalty. Not surprisingly, they eventually declared him emperor.

Julian began his march toward Byzantium to confront Constantius. But Constantius died before their forces could meet.

Then began the reign that gave Julian his place in history. Murdoch notes that Julian did some things extremely well—tax reform, for example, and military leadership. But no one remembers Julian as a tax reformer or even much as a general.

He is remembered as "The Apostate," and Murdoch gives a fascinating analysis of his religious ideas and practical reforms. He made vast sums available to restore temples that had fallen into disrepair over a generation of Christian hegemony. He promoted pagans to prominent positions in the capital and boosted the wages of the pagan priesthoods. He tried, at least in the beginning, to include Christians in his dawning era of toleration; but the Church's big names were wary. Pagan restoration became the keynote of Julian's rule.

Yet, as Murdoch makes clear, Julian's paganism was not really the old religion. It was, rather, a mirror image of Christianity. It was an anti-Church, a reactionary project. Julian himself recognized Christianity's influence on his ideas. You can take the emperor out of the Church, but you can't take the Church out of the emperor. Murdoch says: "Julian's attempts at creating a pagan doctrine betray his Christian upbringing... By the very fact of his early education, he was already, as he would have put it, polluted."

Whereas the old religion had been a riot of gods, cults, and feasts, Julian strove, in a very Roman way, to impose unity and uniformity on worldwide polytheism. It was the religious equivalent of herding cats. In Julian's schema, the emperor himself served as a sort of pope over a hierarchy that mirrored the Catholic structure of metropolitans, bishops, and priests. He set up pagan philanthropies in imitation of Catholic charities. He urged his clergy to lead lives of virtue and preach philosophy to the people. Julian himself had chosen to lead a celibate life after the death of his wife. As Murdoch puts it: "He wanted the pagans to out-Christian the Christians."

His pagan "coming out" climaxed during an extended stay in Syrian Antioch, a city of a half-million people situated en route to the battlegrounds where he would meet the Persians. While in Antioch, Julian renewed the pagan practices, though he was hardly satisfied with the priests' performance.

He showed himself to be as prissy and uptight as any of history's most fanatical puritans—or the most over-educated diocesan liturgist. Murdoch does not miss the irony of a pagan prig enraged by his encounter with a city full of Christian sensualists.

Julian's experience in Antioch led to harsher strictures on Christians. He banned believers from teaching grammar, rhetoric, and philosophy. This, says Murdoch, was Julian's "master stroke." Banished from the public square, Christianity could be minimized as a cultural force. He "had marginalised Christianity to the point where it could potentially have vanished within a generation or two, and without the need for physical coercion."

It was not to last, however. As Julian shook the dust of Antioch from his feet, he marched his troops to their devastating defeat at the hands of Shapur II of Persia. As ever, Murdoch is superb in his systematic yet suspenseful narrative of that miserable campaign.

On that battlefield at the Persian frontier, Julian falls, and with him the Eastern empire begins to crumble. Some (Christian) histories portray the emperor struck by a spear and crying out, "Thou hast won, O Galilean!"

Yet Julian the Apostate lives in our collective memory. For some he is the archetype of the ideological dictator, the bloodless wonk whose ideas justify his bloodletting. For others he is a romantic anti-hero—the rebel against the inevitable. He survives in spite of his utter lack of the qualities that make Nero, Caligula—and even Constantine—perennial subjects of potboiler novels and gory flicks. In contrast to other emperors, Murdoch says, Julian's story bogs down with "an excess of philosophy and too little sex."

For Murdoch, Julian's death was—like the deposition of Romulus—a critical moment in the fall of the empire: "To all intents and purposes we can say that paganism died as a credible political and social force in the last days of June 363."

In ends such as these, Christians found their beginning.

Murdoch's books are not confessionally Christian histories—not in the least. But neither are they the hatchet jobs Christians have come to expect from secular historians in recent centuries. As the agendas of the Reformation and Enlightenment fade, good historians can let the story emerge in bold detail. And Murdoch tells a story as well as the best of them.

"AND WITH YOUR SPIRIT"

THE BIG DIFFERENCE IN A LITTLE PHRASE

A REPORTER CALLED TO INTERVIEW ME about the English translation of the Roman Missal introduced in 2011. We spoke for a while about the process and problems of translation before she asked which of the forthcoming changes I thought would be the most important.

Perhaps too hastily I said it would be the congregation's response to the priest's invocation: "The Lord be with you."

For the last forty years or so, we've been responding with "And also with you."

As of December 2011 we'll say "And with your spirit."

My interviewer asked the intelligent follow-up: "Why?"

I don't remember how I responded, but I'm sure it was some more refined version of the response I usually give to my kids: *Because I said so.*

In the days following, however, I found myself scrutinizing my answer.

It does seem a slight change—the addition of one word, the subtraction of another. But it's actually rather large in its implications.

Indeed, I'm not the only one to notice this. The U.S. bishop most intensely involved with the promotion of the new translation, Cardinal Francis George, has singled out this response as somehow illustrative of the whole project.

But that's not all. The American hierarch who has been most *critical* of the new translation, Bishop Donald Trautman of Erie, has tagged this particular change as problematic—and illustrative of the problems he had with the entire project.

They're two bishops, representing two very different views of the new translation. Yet both agree that this little change, to this little phrase, is important and representative.

So I'd like to examine some reasons why this simple salutation might be so important.

Those reasons, as I see them, fall into five broad categories: *frequency*, *ubiquity*, *antiquity*, *theological weight*, and *liturgical tone*.

1. FREQUENCY. The simplest matter to point out is frequency. We will repeat that phrase more often than any other in the liturgy—*five times* in the course of a typical Sunday Mass. We say it in the introductory rites, at the Gospel, at the beginning of the Eucharistic Prayer, in the Communion rite, and finally in the concluding rites.
2. UBIQUITY. We do this not only in the Latin rite. You'll hear it also (and often) from the Copts in Egypt and Ethiopia, the Chaldeans in Iraq, the Malabars in India, and the Carpatho-Rusyns in the Ukraine. That's ubiquity. Liturgical sound-bytes don't get more universal than "And with your spirit."
3. ANTIQUITY. True catholicity is universality not only in space, but also in time. We Catholics respect what G.K. Chesterton called "the democracy of the dead." And when we study the remnants of Christian antiquity we find that line again and again.

> *The Lord be with you. And with your spirit.*
> *Peace be with you. And with your spirit.*

They represent a common exchange of greetings in Semitic cultures, one evident in the Scriptures and still in use today.

In the Book of Ruth, chapter 2, we read:

> *And behold, Boaz came from Bethlehem; and he said to the reapers, "The Lord be with you!" And they answered, "The Lord bless you."*

In the First Book of Chronicles (22:11, 16), we find King David using this formula in a more solemn way, as he pronounces his final blessing upon his son, Solomon:

> *Now, my son, the Lord be with you, so that you may succeed in building the house of the Lord your God, as he has spoken concerning you . . . Arise and be doing! The Lord be with you!*

In the New Testament letters of St. Paul, we at last find the words cast in the spirited form that will soon be familiar to us. "The Lord be with your spirit" (2 Tim. 4:22). "The grace of the Lord Jesus Christ be with your spirit" (Phil. 4:23).

It seems probable that this greeting was used in the ancient synagogue liturgies of the Jews. From these liturgies the earliest Christians likely adapted the form for the Church's Eucharist.

And it appears often in the ancient Christian witnesses. We find it in *The Apostolic Tradition*, usually attributed to St. Hippolytus of Rome. Though composed around AD 215, the document claims to be setting down the "spiritual gifts" the Church has had "right from the beginning."

The Apostolic Tradition is a manual of "Church order," laying down customs and disciplines related to liturgy and morals. Other Church orders emerged, around this time and a little later, throughout the Christian world. Unanimously they witness to the exchange of greeting in the form we will soon hear at every Mass: "The Lord be with you . . . And with your spirit." "Peace be with you . . . And with your spirit."

We find the exchange in Coptic, Syriac, Greek, and Latin— the liturgies of Jerusalem, Antioch, Rome, Milan, Alexandria, Constantinople, and Edessa. It is in the *Didascalia Apostolorum* and the *Apostolic Constitutions*.

As we turn from the third century to the fourth, we find another form of catechesis beginning to emerge from the shadows. It's called *mystagogy*. Mystagogical preaching explains the deeper meaning of the liturgy's words, postures, and gestures.

The mystagogical homilies of the fourth century, like the Church orders before them, all witness to the frequent use of the traditional exchange: "The Lord be with you. And with your spirit."

Their interpretations, then, bring us to the fourth of the five categories we're considering.

4. THEOLOGICAL WEIGHT. One of those fourth-century preachers, Theodore of Mopsuestia, a Syrian bishop, spoke often of the exchange because it recurred frequently in his liturgy. He spoke of it as a sort of *epiclesis*, an invocation of the Holy Spirit to come down in blessing upon the priest and his people, just as the Spirit comes down upon the offering of bread and wine.

The greeting, then, is more than a "Hi, how are ya?" It's an important moment highlighting the Spirit's power to transform not only the elements offered in the Mass, but also the communicants who partake of the Sacrament. Theodore's interpretation seems to require the presence of the word "spirit."

Theodore's friend and classmate, St. John Chrysostom, went still further in analyzing the exchange. He held that the congregation's response, "And with your spirit," is an implicit profession of faith in the power of the Sacrament of Holy Orders. Chrysostom's claims demand our closest attention.

> *If the Holy Spirit were not in this your common father and teacher, you would not, just now, when he ascended this holy chair and wished you all peace, have cried out with one accord, "And with your spirit."*

> *Thus you cry out to him, not only when he ascends his throne and when he speaks to you and prays for you, but also when he stands at this holy altar to offer the sacrifice. He does not touch that which lies on the altar before wishing you the grace of our Lord, and before you have replied to him, 'And with your spirit.'*

> *By this cry, you are reminded that he who stands at the altar does nothing, and that the gifts that repose there are not the merits of a man; but that the grace of the Holy Spirit is present and, descending on all, accomplishes this mysterious sacrifice. We indeed see a man, but it is God who acts through him. Nothing human takes place at this holy altar.*

Because they are "other Christs," our Catholic priests speak and act with the power of the Holy Spirit. They do so when they repeat that five-time epiclesis: "The Lord be with you." Indeed, only a man who has been ordained may pronounce those words in the liturgy. A layman leading a prayer service may not.

How important is that little exchange? Consider this: in the ninth century, some local churches enacted legislation forbidding the celebration of private Masses. They based their argument on the fact that, in the repeated salutation, the priest addresses worshippers in the plural—dominus vobiscum—and the greeting requires a response in the singular—et cum spiritu tuo. Without a congregation of at least two worshippers in addition to the priest, both sides of the exchange seemed meaningless. The discussion went on for centuries before the Church settled on a consensus in favor of private Masses. The "vobis" addressed by the priest is understood to be all of Christendom.

5. LITURGICAL TONE. And so we come to our last category.

Cardinal George expressed his hope that this small change in wording will bring about a larger change in the way we experience the Mass. At the beginning of the translation project, he wrote in his archdiocesan newspaper: "Our current translation might seem more personal and friendly, but that's the problem."

The spirit referred to in the Latin is the spirit of Christ that comes to a priest when he is ordained, as St. Paul explained to St. Timothy. In other words, the people are saying in their response that Christ as head of the Church is the head of the liturgical assembly, no matter who the particular priest celebrant might be. That is a statement of faith, a statement distorted by transforming it into an exchange of personal greetings.

He's hit on something here. The elimination of the words "your spirit" does seem to reduce the exchange to a common greeting and not much more.

But in the tradition, as we've seen, it is *so* much more. One twentieth-century commentator (Maurice Zundel) spoke of it as a *rallying cry*. The priest issues it as a summons whenever the Church is about to do something new in the liturgy—launch the Mass, proclaim the Gospel, make the offering, or dismiss the faithful to be Christ to the world.

At every new beginning in our Mass, we draw nearer to the divine mystery. We draw closer than Moses was on Mount Sinai, closer than the high priest had been in the Holy of Holies in the Jerusalem Temple. We *need* the Lord to be with us. We need the Spirit of Christ as we advance. Because that's the only way we can be safe, so close to the divine fire.

In our sacramental liturgy, the things of nature are elevated to supernatural significance. It happens with bread. It happens with wine. It happens with common words. They can speak with power that's supernatural, and they can effect what they signify. They don't need great pomp to do this. But clarity and completeness can only help.

Liturgical formality is, of course, no guarantee of congregational reverence. It's funny that in another long passage where St. John Chrysostom unpacks the meaning of "And with your spirit," he also decries the irreverence he witnesses in church every Sunday. In the old days, he pointed out, the houses became churches; now, he said, the churches have become mere houses, where Christians behave with casualness and carelessness, heedless of the divine mystery in their midst.

He continues in an imploring tone: "When I say, 'Peace be unto you,' and you say, 'And with your spirit,' say it not with the voice only, but also with the mind; not in mouth only, but in understanding also."

That should be our rallying cry today. May the Lord indeed be with us!

THE TESTIMONY OF
HOSTILE WITNESSES

WHAT PAGANS HAD TO SAY ABOUT JESUS

AN OBSCURE RABBI FROM A BACKWATER of the Roman Empire, Jesus of Nazareth was hardly a "superstar" by today's standards.

His fame was, for the most part, a local phenomenon. The world and its cultures took little notice of His coming and going. And so it remained for nearly a century.

Jesus' claims to authority—and even divinity—surely would have seemed absurd to the average Roman citizen. A carpenter had come to save the world. He was God, yet He was publicly executed in a most humiliating way. And after a century, the world seemed no more saved than before.

To the most cultured, and to the movers and shakers of the Roman Empire, Jesus didn't matter. He hardly merited a joke or a second glance. But Pope John Paul II believes that was just as it should be.

"This 'becoming one of us' on the part of the Son of God took place in the greatest humility," the pope wrote in *Tertio Millennio Adventiente* ("As the Third Millennium draws near"). "So it is no wonder that secular historians, caught up by more stirring events and by famous personages, first made only passing, albeit significant, references to Him."

Just what "passing" did they take, and why is it "significant"? The pope dedicates a paragraph to these rare testimonies in his long meditation on the incarnation of Christ.

The first he takes up is by Flavius Josephus, the Jewish historian of the Roman Court, who wrote his *Antiquities of the Jews* about sixty to sixty-five years after Christ's death. Josephus' only undisputed reference to Jesus appears as he describes the severity of the Sadducees in judging offenders against the law.

The example he offers is that of the apostle James, "the brother of Jesus, who was called Christ." Yet Josephus is concerned here not with Jesus but with James, who was "delivered to be stoned."

In a footnote, the pope mentions another passage that appears in some manuscripts of *Antiquities of the Jews*, but is missing from others.

Scholars who believe the passage is authentic claim that it had been purged by copyists during times when Christians were persecuted. Those who believe it is false claim it was plugged in by pious copyists of later centuries. The pope, in his footnote, acknowledges the dispute.

The passage comes as Josephus is relating the reign of Pontius Pilate as procurator of Judea. After a description of how Pilate rather violently put down rebellions, the text reads:

> *Now there was about this time Jesus, a wise man, if it be lawful to call him a man, for he was a doer of wonderful works—a teacher of such men as receive the truth with pleasure. He drew over to him both many of the Jew and many of the Gentiles. He was the Christ; and when Pilate, at the suggestion of the principal man amongst us, had condemned him to the cross, those that loved him at the first did not forsake him, for he appeared to them alive again the third day, as the divine prophets had foretold these and 10,000 other wonderful things concerning him; and the tribe of Christians, so named from him, are not extinct at this day.*

The problem some scholars raise (and even some Church fathers raised) is that if Josephus could make a statement of faith such as "He was the Christ," such a faith should pervade the rest of his history—especially his reading of the prophets and patriarchs, and at the very least his reading of the death of St. James. But it doesn't.

In recent centuries, some unbelieving scholars have used the paucity of references to Jesus in Josephus' writings to argue against the Nazarene's very existence. Yet they perhaps forget that Josephus elsewhere proclaims his own master, the Emperor Vespasian, to be the Messiah, and so the historian would probably be reluctant to give notice to the most promising "competition."

In any event, a handful of Romans recorded their brief notice of Jesus and His followers as the years wore on.

Pope John Paul also mentions the historian Tacitus, writing between AD 115 and 120 on the burning of Rome, which Emperor Nero had blamed on the Christians.

Tacitus recorded that the founder of this sect ("hated for their abominations") was one "Christus," who "suffered the extreme penalty during the reign of Tiberius at the hands of one of our procurators, Pontius Pilate."

Christ also appears, by name only, in the "Lives of the Caesars," by the historian Suetonius, writing around AD 121.

Another brief but more telling remark comes in the testimony of Pliny the Younger, writing in AD 111–113 when he was Roman governor of Bithynia, on the Black Sea. Reporting his routine interrogations and torture to Emperor Trajan, Pliny spoke of the Christian sect as something harmless.

They gather once a week, he wrote, "on a designated day, before dawn, to sing in alternating choirs a hymn to Christ as to a God."

The pagan Pliny's report, then, is among the earliest records of orthodox Christology—relating the early Church's belief of the divinity in Christ.

Perhaps the pope could have mentioned more in *Tertio Millennio Adventiente.* For instance, Celsus, an anti-Christian polemicist of around AD 180, never for a moment doubted that Jesus had lived. Rather, he directed his attacks at the divinity of Christ and the veracity of His miracles.

The mother of all early pagan records, perhaps, was by the neoplatonist Porphyry, who wrote fifteen volumes against Christ—again, never denying that He had lived, but taking aim rather at the Church's idea of who and what Jesus was.

Porphyry's nastiness was so offensive to Christians, however, that they fairly thoroughly wiped it out, once they were running the empire. Today, Porphyry is known only from what the Church fathers said in response to him.

It is one of the ironies of history that all those contemporaries who made such passing reference to Christ should themselves become passing references in today's record of that pivotal moment in human history.

In *Tertio Millennio Adventiente,* the pope, after giving a paragraph to Josephus, Suetonius, Tacitus and Pliny, sweeps on to fifty-four paragraphs about Jesus of Nazareth whose birth the world will mark in the year 2000.

Indeed, today the world marks its years from the birthday of that obscure carpenter of so many years ago.

If Catholics can draw a lesson for themselves, maybe it is that they should expect little from today's media and opinion makers—who may be tomorrow's footnotes.

But the truth about history endures in the Lord of History. Jesus Christ is the same, yesterday, today and forever.

THE CARPENTER'S DOZEN

ON THE LIVES OF THE APOSTLES

THEY WERE HISTORY'S MOST ELITE CORPS: twelve men, chosen by God Himself to establish His Church on earth.

Elite, yes. But the apostles, each and all, emerged from obscurity only to do their appointed work, and then faded again into obscurity. "Bartholomew we don't know much about, Matthew almost nothing and Matthias nothing at all," said C. Bernard Ruffin, author of an excellent popular history of the apostles' later years, *The Twelve: The Lives of the Apostles After Calvary* (Our Sunday Visitor, 1998). "None of the apostles seems to have had the slightest interest in perpetuating his own memory. Their whole beings centered on their Master, and on spreading the Good News."

Thus most of what modern Christians know about the Twelve Apostles is what the apostles themselves wrote about the life and teachings of Jesus—the various books of the New Testament. After that, there are snippets, quotations and anecdotes in the documents of the early Church, and legends and oral tradition handed down among the peoples of the Middle East and India. But these are not widely known. Still, they are fascinating to consider. For example:

▷ What happened to Peter's wife (see Mk. 1:29–31)? And what about the couple's children?

▷ What was John's life like when he shared a home with Mary (see Jn. 19:27)?

▷ What did the apostles do to celebrate Easter?

▷ How did a Jew like Thomas take the culture shock that went with evangelizing India?

Ruffin set himself the task of sifting through all the available evidence to answer such questions and compile vivid profiles of the Twelve Apostles and their lives after Jesus' resurrection.

"Few things can be known for sure about events 2,000 years ago," Ruffin told me in an interview about his book. "Yet, as I did my research, I was surprised to find that we know as much as we do, and especially that we have much material that is better than legendary. It comes on very good authority."

Ruffin said that material on Jesus' inner circle—Peter, James and John—is especially plentiful, and recorded by reputable and reliable early Christian authors. St. Polycarp, for example, whose writings survive, knew St. John the Apostle. The writings of Polycarp's disciple, St. Irenaeus, relate many more stories of John. Another "hearer" of John, a bishop named Papias—whose work survives only in fragments—wrote about his master as well as the other apostles. Eusebius and St. Jerome, both historians of the fourth century, drew from these and other first-century documents, now lost, as they wrote their own works.

In addition to these, as we explained earlier, there are also fanciful and apocryphal books of "Acts" of the various apostles—novels, really, but sometimes based on real historical events.

Ruffin's book sometimes reads like a detective story as he pieces stories together from far-flung sources. "A lot of it has to be supposition and guesswork," he told me. "But if you have a number of apparently independent traditions about a certain event, and they're reasonably similar to one another, I think you can be reasonably sure that they're based on a real event."

The chapter on the apostle Thomas provides a good example of Ruffin's investigative technique. Early Church testimonies named Thomas as the apostle to the Far East, including China, but especially India.

"In the West, a number of traditions refer to Thomas's work in India," Ruffin said. "I cite papers in the Edessan archive, which we know from citations in Eusebius in the fourth century. There is more information in the *Doctrine of the Apostles*, a Syrian document from the third century, and the 'Acts of Thomas,' which is one of the apocrypha. Centuries later, Marco Polo and Western missionaries found a number of Thomas traditions in India. The ancient Mar Thoma church, for centuries, has passed down an oral tradition called the *Rabban Song* about Thomas. What is interesting is the degree to which the traditions in India seem to corroborate the traditions from the West."

According to tradition, Thomas received his Indian mission in a vision of Christ. To go to India was, for Thomas, to travel to the end of the earth. It was a place as remote from his native Judea—in terms of geography, culture, climate and especially religion—as one could imagine. Thomas reportedly asked Jesus, "How can I, a Jew, go and preach the Truth to Indians?"

But, according to the *Rabban Song*, preach he did. Through the AD 50s, 60s and early 70s., he brought the Gospel through large areas of the Indian subcontinent, with intermittent success. Legends attribute seventeen thousand conversions to Thomas and his followers in that short time. Ruffin relates the tradition that Thomas was martyred on July 3 in the year 72 by priests of the goddess Kali who feared that the apostle's religion was beginning to eclipse their own.

For years, these traditions were dismissed as folklore. Even some Catholic missionaries charged that ancient heretics invented the Thomas stories in order to fabricate apostolic origins for their teachings. Then, in the last hundred years, archeological discoveries began to confirm some of the historical details of the "Rabban Song" and "Acts of Thomas." In the late nineteenth century, for example, coins were found with the image of a prince who plays a key role in Thomas's story—and his dates correspond with those of Thomas's work in India.

Though Ruffin approaches all ancient documents with caution, he refuses to follow those scholars who dismiss testimony as untrustworthy merely because it is old or because it shows fervor in faith.

"Some scholars tend to be overly skeptical," he said. "In approaching material like this, if you go into the project determined to throw it all out, you probably will persuade yourself to do so. But, then, what's the point of beginning at all?"

Ruffin, a Lutheran pastor who also teaches history, recalled his own experience studying at Yale Divinity School and Bowdoin College. "When

I was in seminary, some of my professors took skepticism to ridiculous extremes," he said. "They were determined to distrust everything, so they did. If we applied the same skepticism to all ancient records that these historians apply to early Christian traditions, we would not only have no Church history, we would have no ancient history at all.

"It comes down to how much value you place on tradition," he concluded. "As a Christian, I think that there are good reasons for us to believe the traditions, even as I acknowledge that not all traditions are of equal weight. Many of the traditions about the apostles do stand scrutiny."

Ruffin's favorite characters in the apostolic corps coincides with Jesus' favorites: Peter, John and James. "Theirs are the most well-documented lives," he said.

Ruffin tells a well-documented story of John, at an advanced age—"maybe 70 or 80," he said—risking his life to save a soul.

"In Smyrna, John had trained a certain young man in the faith. But then came a persecution, and John had to flee. When the apostle came back, he asked the local bishop what had happened to the fellow. At first, he was told that the man was dead. But with further inquiry, he found that the fellow had become a bandit. So John rode out to the back country where the man was hiding out. Soon, he was surrounded by members of the gang. John told the bandits that he wasn't going to escape and he was asking for no mercy, but that he wanted to see their leader.

"When the bandit leader saw John," Ruffin continued, "he turned to run away—but John ran after him! Remember, now, John was very old by this time. He called to the bandit, 'Why are you running from your own father, who is unarmed and very old? Be sorry for me, my child.' And the man fell to the ground sobbing. He repented and returned to the fold. The story showed that John had courage and endurance, even at an advanced age."

Still, in the apostles' biographies, there remains much more shadow than light.

"There are several different traditions about what happened to Matthew," Ruffin said. "Some have him dying in Ethiopia, and some have him dying elsewhere. I labeled his chapter 'The Phantom Apostle,' because I can't figure out what happened to him."

Yet even the questionable material is valuable, he explained, because "it shows us the qualities that the early Christians esteemed above all others. Some of their stories may be metaphorical, describing more a spiritual state than a historical event. But I don't think we should approach these cultures in a condescending way, explaining them away as prescientific storytellers."

Most fascinating to modern Catholic readers, perhaps, will be the degree to which the apostles' Church mirrors the Catholic Church today—in its sacraments, ritual, hierarchy, dogma and even its foibles.

But that shouldn't be surprising at all. Ruffin cited St. Irenaeus, of the second century AD, who "maintained that the apostles had 'perfect knowledge' and maintained that they appointed bishops to whom they passed on their sacred mysteries."

THE SENSES OF CHRISTMAS

CHRISTMAS COULD RIGHTLY BE CALLED the holiday of the senses.

It is the season of lights and tinsel, choirs and carols, the aroma of pine and roasting chestnuts. Christmas comes to us with sumptuous meals, hearty laughter, and kisses beneath the mistletoe. Christmas scenes—by the old masters and by modern advertisers—decorate the walls of museums, billboards on the roadside, and cards in the mailbox. For nearly two thousand years, the world has marked the birth of Jesus Christ as its most festive jubilee. No other day of the year offers the world so many earthly pleasures.

But why? No pope or Church council ever declared that it should be so. Yet every year, Christmas comes onto the calendar like a sudden December wind, like the blinding sun reflected off new snow. It is a shock to the senses, to go from barren winter to the season of lights and feasting.

And so it should be, for the first Christmas—the day when Jesus Christ was born—was a shock to human history.

For millennia, humankind had lived and died, uncomprehending, in its sin, the miseries of this world inevitable and the joys few and fleeting. Then Christmas arrived, and even the calendar went mad. From that moment, all of history was cleft in two: before that day (BC), and after that day (AD). The world—with all its sights and sounds and aromas and embraces—was instantly transfigured. For the world's redemption had begun the moment God took human flesh for His own, the moment God was born in a poor stable in Bethlehem.

The greatest Christian poem commemorates this moment when God definitively came to dwell on earth. St. John begins his Gospel by describing a God of awesome power, remote in space and transcending time: a Spirit, a Word: "In the beginning was the Word, and the Word was with God, and the Word was God. He was in the beginning with God; all things were made through Him."

This is the God that even the pagan philosophers knew: the Prime Mover, the One, the Creator. Yet, precisely where the pagan philosophers stalled, John's drama proceeded to a remarkable climax: "And the Word was made flesh, and dwelt among us."

This was shocking news. From the distant heavens, from remotest time, God Himself had come in flesh to "pitch His tent" among His people. Yes, God is eternally the Word, but a word is elusive, and not everyone may grasp it. Now He is also a baby, and a baby may be picked up and held and embraced.

Of all the amazing and confounding truths of the Christian religion, there is none so outrageous as this: that the Word was made flesh, in a particular little town, in a stable filled with animals, on a certain day of the year. The Word was made flesh and changed everything. This makes Christmas the most shocking feast in the calendar.

And all the meaning of Christmas is summed up in this fact. God lived in a family the way we do. He shivered against the cold the way we do. The Word-made-flesh nursed at His mother's breast like any other human baby. Suddenly, God was not a watchmaker, some remote mechanic who wound up the world and let it go. God was a baby, crying to be picked up.

Tradition tells us that John wrote the Prologue to his Gospel in a white heat of inspiration. His friends had asked him to set down the story of Jesus, so he asked them a favor in return: to fast and pray with him. When the fast was over, the Spirit came upon John, and he could not contain himself. The words poured out—perhaps the very words he had been trying to say all his long life, but had never quite managed to find before.

You can hear the astonishment in his voice when he tells us that the Word was made flesh. As he was writing, he must have felt that same thrill again, the thrill he felt when it first hit home that this Jesus, the carpenter from Nazareth, was the Anointed, the Son of God.

And that same astonishment carries over into his first epistle. According to tradition, John wrote that letter sixty-six years after the Ascension of Christ, but the amazement is still fresh in his voice. He still can hardly believe that "that which was from the beginning" is also that "which we have heard, which we have seen with our eyes, which we have looked upon and touched with our hands" (1 Jn. 1:1)

IN THE EARLIEST DAYS OF THE CHURCH, Christmas was not one of the important feasts. Jesus' life was still a living memory, and His extraordinary Resurrection rightly occupied the central spot in the calendar. But as time went on, false teachers began to deny the fact of Jesus' humanity. They claimed that Jesus' body had been an elaborate disguise, that, in reality, God had never debased Himself by taking on human flesh. Later heretics denied also that Mary gave birth to the Word: instead, they said, she gave birth to a "vessel" into which the Word was later poured. Still other heretics believed that the Son was a subordinate being—divine, but not coeternal with God the Father.

All these heresies had one thing in common: an unwillingness to face the apparent foolishness of the Incarnation. Arius, the founder of the Arian heresy, was an eminently reasonable man. He denied the doctrine of the Trinity because, he said, three cannot be one; that's elementary arithmetic. The infinite God cannot become finite man; that's elementary philosophy. Therefore there could be no Incarnation.

Heretics like Arius wanted to spare God the unreasonable indignity of being corrupted by too close an association with humanity. It was the same problem the Pharisees could not get over: If this Jesus is so good, why does He associate with sinners and tax collectors? In fact, though the heretics would have insisted that they were defending the perfection of the Deity, they were actually denying the perfection of God's love. Love, after all, can seem unreasonable. Anyone who values another as much as oneself seems entirely unreasonable.

It can hardly be coincidence that the celebration of the literal, historical birth of Jesus the carpenter's son began to take on more importance just when the true Faith was most dangerously beset by these flesh-denying errors. The scandalously human birth of the Son of God was the very thing that separated orthodoxy from heresy. Celebrating that Nativity committed the Church to a clear statement of principle.

IN THE BEGINNING, THERE WAS NO UNIVERSAL AGREEMENT on the date of Christmas. The Church in Egypt at first placed the date of Christ's birth in May or April. Others put it in March, and still others in any other month you care to name. It was also popular to combine the celebration of Christ's birth with the celebration of the Epiphany, putting them both on January 6. But sometime in the 400s the date of the Feast of the Incarnation settled on December 25, and there it stayed.

There are at least three plausible theories to account for how Christmas came to be celebrated on December 25. No one of the theories excludes the others; all three could be correct.

The first theory is the simplest. An old story says that in about the year 350 Pope Julius I looked up the date of Jesus' birth in the census records. Certainly there is nothing outlandish in the idea of census records holding that information even three and a half centuries later. We know from Luke's Gospel that Jesus was born during a census. The Romans, with their almost compulsive love of order, might well have kept those records forever in some bureaucratic hole in Rome.

The second theory has it that Christians, unable to stamp out a pagan midwinter celebration, simply took it over. Throughout history, people have celebrated the passing of the shortest day in the year, the solstice. When the days begin to lengthen again, it means that the death of winter will certainly pass, and the world will be reborn in spring.

The pagan origin of the date should not scandalize us. Indeed, many Christmas traditions have pagan origins. The Christmas tree, for example, has no obvious connection with the birth of Jesus, but certainly makes sense as a pagan midwinter rite: By sympathetic magic, we bring back the dormant spirit of vegetation when we bring an evergreen tree—still living when everything around it is dead—back from the forest. And yet it is an appropriate symbol for Christians, too. The evergreen tree is an obvious metaphor for the hope of new life that Christ brought us.

Again, the lights we string everywhere for Christmas may be a survival of an old heathen rite—once again, a kind of sympathetic magic, lighting fires to bring the dying sun back to life. But light has always been a favorite Christian symbol, too.

We know that the early Church frequently took advantage of local beliefs or customs to spread the Gospel. Paul himself founded one of his most famous orations on the altar to an unknown god in Athens. "What therefore you worship as unknown," he told the gawking Athenians, "this I proclaim to you" (Acts 17:23). It would be very much in the spirit of Paul for the Church to develop a Christian interpretation of a beloved heathen festival, explaining to eager converts that they were really worshipping not the light, but the Light.

The third theory to account for the specific date December 25 is that it corresponded with the early Church's notion of Jesus' perfect life. Tradition had it that Jesus died on March 25. In order for His life to be appealingly perfect, the theologians reasoned, He must also have been conceived on March 25, then born exactly nine months later.

The idea of Jesus' life having a kind of aesthetic perfection must have been satisfying to an age still under the spell of Neoplatonist philosophy. It would have satisfied the intellect, and that Roman passion for order, as much as the continuation of the beloved midwinter festival satisfied the sentiments.

All of these theories could be true. One can imagine, for example, the pope discovering the date in census records, and the Church taking advantage of its happy correspondence with the date of a favorite pagan festival, even as the more philosophical Christians capitalized on its appealing symmetry with the traditional date of Jesus' death. As always, Christians would have reached out to the nations in ways the nations were prepared to hear. By giving a Christian interpretation to a favorite local custom or an appealing philosophical idea, the Church gave the newly converted a way of seeing the story of the Incarnation in terms they could understand.

AS THE FESTIVAL SPREAD throughout the newly Christianized nations of Europe and the East, it gathered more old pagan customs and gave them new Christian interpretations. Everywhere Christmas went, it must have seemed new but somehow familiar to newly converted pagans. Perhaps that very familiarity made it the most beloved feast in the calendar.

At any rate, by about 1100, Christmas had become the most important celebration of the year. Throughout the high Middle Ages, Christmas was celebrated everywhere with tremendous spectacles and rejoicing. The people sang their favorite carols; psychedelic processions wound noisily through the narrow streets of medieval cities; and everywhere there was the heavenly aroma of Christmas cooking.

With the Protestant Reformation, however, came changes on the cultural scene. In their zealous rage against any perceived abuses in the Church, many of the Reformers targeted Christmas as nothing more than a mishmash of heathen festivals. In a sense, of course, they were correct: many of the traditions did come from pagan roots. But the anti-Christmas factions judged by the stem when they ought to have judged by the fruit.

When the Puritans took over in England, they banned Christmas outright. Shops were ordered to stay open. Anyone caught with a mince pie was in serious trouble. All the greenery, Yule logs, plum puddings, and carols that make up a traditional English Christmas were (the Puritans said) nothing but heathen idolatry, and heathen idolatry must be suppressed. There were stubborn pockets of resistance—some people were even willing to die for Christmas, so strong was the popular attachment to the traditional holiday—but the Puritans prevailed, though only for a while.

To counteract all that heathen wallowing in sensory pleasures, the Puritans decreed that Christmas would be a day of fasting. Somehow that tradition never caught on. It would be easy to say that the fast never caught on because of human weakness—people, after all, prefer feasting to fasting almost as naturally as they prefer joy to sorrow. But Lent never dropped out of the calendar from lack of demand. Good Christians are willing to endure self-denial when it seems appropriate. It just does not seem appropriate for Christmas.

What the Puritans could not understand, and what many good people still fail to understand, is that there is no contradiction between worshipping

God and enjoying God's creation. It is no shame to enjoy the good things God has given us. Jesus' first recorded miracle was turning water into wine—and not just ordinary wine, St. John is careful to point out that this was the good stuff. Apparently, the Son of Man had, in the most human and fleshly sense, good taste.

Some misguided Christians, like the Puritans, are ashamed to sully the affairs of faith with earthly enjoyment. But the miracle of Christ's birth is that it was earthly. The Word became flesh—real, unmistakably earthly flesh. "Flesh," said St. Athanasius, the heroic champion of orthodoxy when the clouds of heresy seemed blackest, "did not diminish the glory of the Word; far be the thought. On the contrary, it was glorified by Him."

The Church fathers called Christmas the Feast of the Incarnation.

Incarnation comes from a Latin word that means "enfleshment." What sounds to English-speakers like a rarefied theological term is really just a statement of fact: God took on flesh. When that happened, flesh itself became something holy, something to be celebrated with paintings and statues and Christmas cards.

Yet in the eighth century, a faction arose in the Church calling themselves "Iconoclasts," Greek for "picture-smashers." The iconoclasts tried to "purify" and "spiritualize" Christian life by obliterating all artistic representations of Jesus, Mary, and the saints. They seized and destroyed most of the religious images in the Eastern Roman Empire, and they cut off the hands of those Christians who would not part with their icons. God, they said, could not be represented in a picture; any attempt to do so was rank idolatry. But this is how St. John of Damascus answered them: "In former times, God, being without form or body, could in no way be represented. But today, since God has appeared in the flesh and lived among men, I can represent what is visible in God. I do not worship matter, but worship the creator of matter Who became matter for my sake . . . and Who, through matter, accomplished my salvation" (*Apology* 1.16).

In other words, the Incarnation makes art, too, a holy thing, just as it made the body a holy thing. The artists who have painted the Nativity throughout the centuries were not creating idols. Their visible representations are hymns of praise to the invisible God made visible.

Look at any of the classic Nativity paintings and marvel at the care taken with the tiniest details. Every animal in the stable is an individual creature; every straw in the manger seems to be drawn with infinite care. Of all the biblical scenes artists have loved to paint for centuries, the Nativity is the one that seems to provoke the most thorough delight in the simple pleasure of drawing things. It seems as if God is in every detail.

EVERYONE'S FAVORITE CHRISTMAS STORY is the one in Luke's Gospel. What makes it so beloved is the familiarity of it all. Luke, who seems to have been writing for a gentile audience, strives to place Jesus exactly in history and geography. His point is that the birth of the Christ is not a metaphor or parable (something a sophisticated Mediterranean audience, accustomed to hearing the philosophers and sophists reinterpret classical mythology allegorically, would easily be tempted to suppose). It was a real event in a real place, related in a precisely knowable way to the other real events of recent history.

Having established the exact time and place, Luke goes on to give us, with a professional historian's skill, exactly the details we need to bring home to the earthly reality of Jesus' birth. We learn how Joseph and Mary felt when they found there was no room at the inn, and how grateful they were for even the scant shelter of a stable—not because Luke tells us how they felt, but because he gives us just enough detail to put us right there with them, and we can feel it for ourselves. Probably no one could ever make a movie out of those events that would really convince us: We were there, we know what it was like, and whatever we saw on the screen or on the stage would never seem half so real.

The other Gospel writers do not provide the same details. They have their own points to make, each one as valuable as Luke's—but not so immediately appealing to our sentimental side.

Mark is the only one who has nothing to say about Jesus' birth. His compact and economical narrative begins with John the Baptist and wastes no time getting Jesus baptized by him.

Matthew tells us only that Jesus was born in Bethlehem, then skips straight to the Wise Men. Matthew and Luke seem to have been writing for different audiences: Matthew for people who had heard of or seen Jesus the man and needed to know that He was also Jesus the Christ, and Luke for people who had heard of Jesus the Christ and needed to be told that He was also Jesus the man.

And then there is John. He actually tells the same story as Luke, but in words so different that at first we do not recognize the story at all. We could almost say that where Luke saw the events from earth's point of view, John saw them from heaven's. Luke gives us the details that let us see the earthliness of the Incarnation; John gives us the poetry that lets us see the miracle of it all.

IT IS IMPORTANT TO HAVE JOHN'S DIVINE WORDS IN MIND when we read the story in Luke, because the Incarnation was not a one-time event that ended on the Cross or with the Ascension. Jesus Christ came into the world in a particular place at a particular time, but He established a Church that would be His body in the world. The gloriously diverse congregation of believers who inhabit every corner of our planet—they are Christ's body. If you want to know what Jesus looks like, go to church and look around you.

Even more, we encounter the Lord in the flesh in the Holy Eucharist. "For My flesh is real food," He said, "and My blood real drink." The Incarnation is not an abstract principle—it is a miraculous concrete fact every day of our lives. It didn't just happen two thousand years ago. It happens today.

The "Incarnational principle"—that embodiment of love—is present in all the sacramental realities Jesus gave us. It is not simply for the sake of weak human understandings that all the sacraments are celebrated with physical signs. God the Son made the physical sacred.

In the Holy Eucharist itself, we see the nourishment for our spirits expressed in the most elementary form of nourishment for the body. The eternal God appears to us in the very temporal form of bread and wine. "This is My body, broken for you," Our Lord told us. "This is My blood, shed for you." As often as we celebrate the Eucharist, we are roused to remember that Jesus the Son of God had real flesh to break and real blood to shed.

That fact is what the Feast of the Incarnation celebrates, and it is what makes enjoying the pleasures of the senses feel so appropriate for Christmas. Throughout His earthly ministry, Jesus of Nazareth healed the sick and fed the hungry. He loved us not just enough to take us with Him into paradise, but to wish us every happiness while we still live here on Earth. And the only thing He asked us to do in return was to love Him, and to love others as much as He loved us.

You can still see traces of that Christian love in the ancient and beautiful custom of giving Christmas presents. There is more than a little irony in the fact that today's manic rush to buy and sell Christmas exists only because we have managed to pervert the beautiful Christian urge to give. That perversion is the very sin that Jesus Himself condemned most angrily when He drove the moneychangers out of the Temple, the only sin that could have driven Him to use a whip on the sinners. What does Jesus think when He sees our "Sparkle Season," the modern midwinter festival of greed? Perhaps (for Jesus is more perfectly forgiving than we could ever be) He sees the good in us, and the earnest desire many of us have to make others happy, and forgives us our excesses. We should pray that it might be so.

But we should not be ashamed to enjoy the beautiful traditions of Christmas, the delights of the senses that go naturally with the season. Eat, drink, sing, laugh, dance, come in before His presence with exceeding great joy. Why, after all, do we have bodies?

"Man, though made of body and soul, is a unity," says the Catechism of the Catholic Church. "Through his very bodily condition he sums up in himself the elements of the material world. Through him they are thus brought to their highest perfection and can raise their voice in praise freely given to the Creator. For this reason man may not despise his bodily life. Rather he is obliged to regard his body as good and to hold it in honor since God has created it and will raise it up on the last day" (CCC 364).

This is what Jesus taught us: We have bodies so that we can use them to worship God, as Jesus of Nazareth did. We have bodies so that we can use them to serve others, as Jesus of Nazareth did. We have bodies so that we can bring comfort and consolation and healing, as Jesus of Nazareth did. We have bodies for glory's sake.

And Christmas is full of that glory. The Gloria, the song of Christmas, comes to us from the Christmas Eve mass of the ancient Church. The angels sang it when they announced Christ's birth: Glory to God in the highest! What was so glorious? This Jesus was born to a poor working family in a drafty stable filled with smelly animals. And that is precisely what was so glorious. There was nothing idealized about Jesus' birth. The Son of God was born in an absolutely ordinary way. The first people to hear of the miracle were certain poor shepherds—not the great and mighty Emperor Augustus in his palace at Rome, not even that two-bit local tin-plated despot Herod. That is the wonder of the Word-made-flesh: the Word was truly made one of us.

The jubilee story—of the world's first Christmas—is the story of how the flesh became holy, the body was sanctified, and simple earthly joys became hymns of praise to God. This book is all about the feast of the jubilee: a feast for the eyes, the ears, and all the senses. We love to hear the story over and over, and we always will love it so long as a scrap of humanity remains in us.

AT THE CROSS ROADS

THE HISTORY AND THE HEART OF THE STATIONS OF THE CROSS

THE WAY OF THE CROSS IS THE INEVITABLE WAY of a Christian's heart.

Indeed, it is almost impossible to imagine the Church without the devotion that goes by that name.

It goes by other names, too: "The Stations of the Cross," "Via Crucis," "Via Dolorosa"—or just "the stations."

The practice has settled, for several centuries now, into brief meditations on fourteen scenes from the suffering and death of Jesus Christ.

Why are Christians drawn so strongly to this devotion? Because Jesus wanted us to be. "Then he said to all, 'If any man would come after me, let him deny himself and take up his cross daily and follow me'" (Lk. 9:23).

When Jesus speaks the words "if" or "unless," Christians listen carefully. For then Our Lord is laying down the conditions of our discipleship—the prerequisites of heaven.

THE WAY OF THE CROSS DEVELOPED GRADUALLY in the life of the Church. In the Roman world, the Cross was a "stumbling block" (Galatians 5:11). Crucifixion was a most humiliating form of execution: a man was stripped naked and suspended in a public place; he was pelted with rocks and trash and left to suffocate slowly while passersby mocked his agony.

Crucifixion was still a common occurrence during the first three centuries of Christianity, so it was not easy for believers, like St. Paul, to "boast" (Gal 6:14) of the Cross. For people who had seen criminals crucified, the Cross could not have been an easy thing to love.

Yet love it they did. Devotion to the Cross pervades the earliest Christian writings. And the earliest records of pilgrimage show us that Christians endured great hardships—traveling thousands of miles, from France and Spain to Jerusalem—so that they could walk the streets of Jesus' suffering: the Way of the Cross.

The Jerusalem liturgy of Holy Week memorialized the events of Jesus' Passion. On Holy Thursday, the bishop led the procession from the Garden of Gethsemane to Calvary.

After Christianity was legalized in AD 313, pilgrims regularly thronged Jerusalem. The Way of the Cross became one of the standard routes for pilgrims and tourists. It wound its way through narrow streets, from the site of Pilate's Praetorium to the summit of Calvary to the sepulcher where Jesus was laid to rest.

How did they know the sites of these events? One ancient story holds that the Virgin Mary continued to visit those places, every day for the rest of her life. Surely, the apostles and the first generation would hold dear the memories of Jesus' Passion and pass them on.

Very likely, the route emerged from the oral history of Palestinian Christians and from the ambitious archeological excavations of the devout empress Helena. Along the way, pilgrims and guides paused at several places traditionally associated with biblical scenes—such as Jesus' conversation with the women of Jerusalem (Lk. 23:27–31)—as well as some scenes not recorded in the Bible. These occasional pauses were known in Latin as *stationes*. By the eighth century, they were a standard part of the Jerusalem pilgrimage.

SUCH PILGRIMAGES GREW IN POPULARITY well into the age of the crusaders. Gradually, the stations became more developed. In fact, history records many different series, varying in number, content and form.

In 1342, the Church entrusted the Franciscan order with the care of the holy sites, and it was these friars who most ardently promoted the praying of the Way of the Cross. Around this time, the popes began to grant indulgences to anyone who devoutly prayed the stations in Jerusalem. Also at this time, the Franciscans began to spread the Marian hymn that would eventually be most closely associated with the devotion: the Latin Stabat Mater, familiarly rendered in English beginning with the words:

At the cross, her station keeping,
Stood the mournful mother weeping,
Close to Jesus to the last.

The lyric is attributed to a Franciscan, Jacopone da Todi, who died in 1306.

European pilgrims were so impressed by the Jerusalem tour that they took the Way home with them. Around the fifteenth century they began to build symbolic replicas of the stations in the churches and monasteries of their homelands. Eight stations had been standard in Jerusalem, but these expanded to as many as thirty-seven in Europe.

The practice became enormously popular. Now everyone—small children, the poor, the infirm—could make their spiritual pilgrimage to Jerusalem, to the Way of the Cross. In a tangible way, they could take up their cross—just as Jesus had commanded—and follow Him to the end.

In the seventeenth and eighteenth centuries, the Stations of the Cross, now settled at fourteen, were considered almost standard equipment in a church building. Some were elaborate—dramatic, life-sized wood carvings of the human figures. Others were mere roman numerals—I through XIV—carved into the church wall at intervals. The popes extended the indulgences customary for Jerusalem pilgrims to Christians everywhere, if they prayed the stations in their own churches in the prescribed way.

The stations continued to be associated with the Franciscan order, and Church law often required that stations be installed (or at least blessed) by a Franciscan priest.

"IF ANY MAN WOULD COME AFTER ME, let him deny himself and take up his cross daily and follow me." Jesus said this to "all," to every Christian. In the earliest days of the Church, it was perhaps easier to know the gravity of His command. The Cross was not yet a symbol. It was a horror that took place, with some frequency, at the edges of town. It was the worst death they could imagine, devised by people who possessed a certain genius for torture.

When Christianity became the official religion of the empire, crucifixion was outlawed. Over time, the most basic Christian devotion—devotion to the Cross of Jesus—began to require an act of imagination.

Today, our need is greater still. For we have sanitized even ordinary death: shutting it up in hospitals, silencing its agonies with drugs. The shame, the gore, and the stench—the commonplaces of public executions—have become incomprehensible. This is the cost of our everyday sins, and yet it is a sum, like the national debt, that is so remote from us that we cannot get worked up over it.

If we pray the Way of the Cross, we cannot help but get worked up. Through the stations we draw near, in our hearts and minds, our intellect and will and imagination, to the scenes beheld by our ancestors. We see a young man scourged with coarse leather whips studded with shards of pottery. His bleeding shoulders, with every nerve raw and exposed, receive a rough wooden beam, heavy enough to hold a man's dead weight. He totters under the weight amid a jeering crowd. Delirious, He weaves along the cobblestones and stumbles, now crushed downward by the wood on His shoulders. His fall gives Him no rest, as the crowd mocks Him by kicking Him, stepping on His raw wounds, spitting in His face. He will fall again and again. When at last He reaches His destination, His torturers pierce the nerves in His hands with nails, affixing Him to the crossbeam, and then raise Him up, placing the beam atop another, thicker beam set perpendicular to the ground. His weakened torso slumps forward, compressing His diaphragm, making it impossible for Him to breathe. To take a breath, He must push up on the nail in His feet or pull up on the nails that pierce His arms. Every breath will cost Him an extremity of pain, until He succumbs to shock or suffocation or blood loss.

This is the hard part of Christianity: our faith cannot exist apart from devotion to the Cross. Our ancestors longed to touch the relics of the true Cross. Even our separated brethren love to survey the old rugged Cross.

It all seems unbearable. But Christ has borne it, and He insisted that we must, too. We cannot be lifted up to heaven except by way of the Cross. Tradition has mapped out the way for us.

AFTERWORD

WHERE THE FASCINATIONS BEGINS

WHEN I WAS A KID, my parents had an old, battered and tattered Family Bible, in the back of which was a long list of saints. I was fascinated by the entry for St. Aquilina. It was nothing but her name, of course—but her name was my name, and I was not accustomed to seeing my last name in lights. At eight years old, living in an immigrant ghetto in small-town Pennsylvania, I couldn't imagine a time or a place where people observed naming conventions that were different from my own. (Even Jesus had a last name, right? Jesus *Christ*.) What's more, I could hardly imagine a Church where all the important people didn't have names like McCormick, Hafey, and Hannan.

Yet here was this little-girl saint, who apparently went by her last name, which happened to be my last name—a last name that ended in a vowel.

My distant cousin, my *paesan*, St. Aquilina had made it to the back pages of a Catholic Bible, printed by an Irish-American publisher. I don't recall whether I fantasized about a *Da Vinci Code*-style bloodline transmitting fortitude across the centuries, but I might have.

Fast-forward many years to the advent of the World Wide Web. When my son first taught me how to surf, he plugged in our surname to impress me with a vanity search. And who should we find but my long-lost cuz, St. Aquilina, the child martyr of Byblos, Lebanon. The Maronite Research Institute had built up an impressive virtual shrine of scholarship in her honor, all sumptuously illustrated. (It now resides on Wikipedia.)

She's not a Father. She never even reached the age to be a mother! But she lived in the patristic era, and so she lives within the purview of this book, and she's worth getting to know.

Aquilina was born in Byblos toward the end of the third century. Like Catholic kids today, she learned her catechism. But she didn't stop at being a good student. When she was twelve, she began to speak to her pagan neighbors about the Christian faith. Her words bowled them over because they flowed from a good life and innocence of soul. Aquilina made many friends, and she made them for Christ. Under her influence, they asked for baptism.

This made some pagan parents furious, and they looked upon Aquilina as a menace. When persecution began to heat up, they seized the opportunity and denounced her before a magistrate. Professing Christianity was, after all, a crime punishable by death—a sentence backed up by two centuries of Roman legal precedent.

In court, Aquilina admitted without hesitation: "I am Christian."

The magistrate fumed, "You are leading your friends and companions away from the religion of our gods to the belief in Christ, the crucified. Don't you know that our kings condemn this Christ and sentence to death those who worship Him? Leave this error and offer sacrifice to the gods, and you shall live. But, if you refuse, you shall undergo the most atrocious sufferings" (St. Aquilina, Wikipedia).

You can guess where this story is going. She was executed on June 13 in the year 293.

Today, St. Aquilina is to the Eastern churches what St. Agnes is to the West: an icon of Christian innocence crushed under the heel of a hostile pagan world.

But is she really my cousin? Well, as far as I know, no one's drawn DNA from her relics, so I can't say for sure. But she is family, because she and I were born from the same mother Church. I like to share her story with my kids. Now I've shared it with you—and you're family, aren't you?

I hope we all live up to the name.